CHINESE
STYLE

the art of living
CHINESE STYLE

BRADLEY QUINN

foreword by Ou Baholyodhin
special photography by Jan Baldwin

First published in 2002 by
Conran Octopus Limited
a part of Octopus Publishing Group
2–4 Heron Quays, London E14 4JP
www.conran-octopus.co.uk

This paperback edition published in 2005

Publishing director: Lorraine Dickey
Senior editor: Muna Reyal
Editor: Alison Wormleighton

Creative director: Leslie Harrington
Design: Megan Smith and Lucy Gowans
Photographer: Jan Baldwin
Stylist: Lyndsay Milne
Senior picture researcher: Rachel Davies
Calligraphy artist: Su Ling Wang

Senior production controller: Manjit Sihra

British Library Cataloguing-in-Publication Data.
A catalogue record for this book is available from
the British Library.

ISBN 1 84091 459 9

Printed in China

contents

FOREWORD

The principal decorative features of the Chinese interior are contemplated in terms of their natural beauty. The wood-grain of timber provided muted, unassuming textures, while the smooth patterns of stone floor tiles enhanced the rich brown and red tones of the woodwork. This formula has remained unchanged for several hundred years, creating settings as distinctive in the twenty-first century as they were in the fourteenth-century Ming interior. Contemporary designers such as Ou Baholyodhin, who designed this interior and Hong Kong chair, create dramatic visions of modern elegance by drawing upon the simplicity of Chinese style.

My first childhood design-conscious memory is of the dramatic, classical Chinese Dragon column carved out of solid rosewood and set within a sleek modernist interior of my grand parents mid-century home in Bangkok. Such unexpected theatrical juxtaposition of two culturally diverse symbols was my initiation to a strain of accidental post-modernism, and more significantly, an early instance of contemporary east meets west.

I have always been intrigued by Chinese style's staying power – how it has managed to remain so hip throughout the last three centuries and still cast an influence today, perhaps more strongly than ever.

Chinese style has become de rigueur in private residences as well as public spaces. The proof is in the ubiquitous pair of antique Chinese chairs or an antique Chinese lacquer chest of some description in just about every issue of a contemporary interior design magazine.

On a more subtle level, we owe much of the sensibility in the approach to contemporary design to the Chinese tradition of cultural refinement and their understanding of nature. Indeed, the emphasis on the importance of spirituality and well being in the contemporary interior is very much a Chinese concept.

Many of us, myself included, do not really appreciate the profound meanings of yin and yang, the intricacies of *qi*, the complexity of feng shui, but somehow we can recognize the harmony of a simple, but perfectly formed contemporary ceramic vase or the poise and tranquillity of an east-meets-west modern interior. Such intricate studies, although complex in formulation, have roots so sensitively grounded and are so primal that they consequently come to us naturally. The modern use of natural materials and surfaces, the preference for simplicity over contrived is so akin to the philosophy of Ming scholars and artisans.

Chinese style is so accessible to all of us; it brings warmth and exoticism to our homes whilst fulfilling our perpetual longing for travel and adventure.

Ou Baholyodhin

INTRODUCTION

A celebrated Tang poet of the eighth century wrote, 'Heavy over distant peaks, only sky limits the emperor's earthly reign. Dare we ever dream of a world beyond this one? Here, among men, lies the enchanted middle kingdom.' To the Chinese their land has always been the middle kingdom. Not merely a vast empire stretching between two oceans and the steppes of Asia, but a realm between heaven and earth inhabited by humans of such refinement that they could only describe the cultures existing outside their domain as 'barbaric'. The belief that their land bridges heaven and earth was so deeply etched upon the minds and values of the Chinese people that their society evolved to mirror heavenly aspirations and express incredibly subtle beauty in art, furniture, ceramics and architecture.

For centuries, Chinese style has caught the imagination of the West. A civilization like that of the Chinese has never existed anywhere else: the mixture of philosophy, scholarship, ceremony and fine art that flourished for centuries created one of the most heavily aestheticized societies the world has ever known. To the ancient Chinese, the home was inextricably bound to a reverence for nature and a fundamental, almost superstitious, belief that balance and harmony must be achieved in the interior. Colours, symbolism, form and function were carefully considered to create objects and images that performed aesthetic as well as practical roles. Each dynasty developed a signature style; each applied purity of form to all aspects of design and emphasized exquisite craftsmanship, leaving a legacy of designs, shapes and elegant motifs that still appear timeless today.

Even before the first decorative works made by Oriental cultures were brought to Europe, the exotic East seemed enigmatic, alluring and mysterious. From the thirteenth century, the extraordinary tales of explorers like Marco Polo described an intriguing and romantic fantasy land called Cathay, where fiery dragons moved amidst palaces and pagodas that were inhabited by exquisite concubines and moustachioed mandarins. These legends of splendour and adventure fired the European imagination, creating a fascination for all things Chinese and an insatiable demand for vestiges of life in that mystic land.

Trade between East and West had always been sporadic, and the land of Cathay was largely presumed to be myth rather than reality. When the port city of Canton (Guangzhou) opened to the West in the seventeenth century, merchant adventurers returned with cargos of porcelain, silk, lacquer and tea, bringing with

Hand-painted with delicate, adept brush strokes and subtle applications of colour, this wallpaper depicting courtly gentlemen captures a mood of scholarly debate. Composition details such as the rock and the bamboo tree evoke Taoist sentiments of wisdom and virtue, while fans depicted in portraits often denoted rank.

them promises of even more resplendent goods to come. Though the traders bore proof that Cathay did exist, the romantic speculation and fantastic visions of pleasure and opulence had already taken hold. Merchants embellished their stock with tales so fantastic that Europeans remained spellbound for two centuries.

By the beginning of the eighteenth century, the widespread enthusiasm for Chinese objects had grown to affect almost every decorative art found in the interior. Furniture, wallpaper, silk hangings, lacquerwares and ceramics featured whimsical motifs of men with embroidered robes and diadem hats, willowy ladies in flowing gowns, performing acrobats, latticed temples and pagodas, mythological animals and trailing flowers. At first only a handful of these decorative objects had found their way to Europe, brought by the crews of trading ships from the East India Company, who were sent primarily to purchase tea and raw silk. The growing demand therefore led European craftsmen to attempt their own imitations of Chinese decorative styles, recklessly using virtually any motif culled from the East, whether it was known to be Chinese or not. As more envoys visited Asia, greater authenticity did become possible, but fantasy seemed to be more appealing to the European taste.

The French court became devoted to the Chinese style, dubbing it 'chinoiserie', which led to its popularity in other parts of Europe. During the seventeenth century, Chinese style became assimilated into the prevailing taste for Baroque. While the Baroque incorporated chinoiserie into its general fascination with the exotic, the craftsmen of the Rococo period, the predominant style of the first half of the eighteenth century, found that chinoiserie decoration captured the essence of European Rococo perfectly. Both diverged from Classical concepts of symmetry and restraint – as the Rococo turned its back on Classical features, the naturalistic motifs and asymmetrical patterns of chinoiserie inspired many of its designs. Although chinoiserie is considered characteristic of the Rococo style, it remained popular even after the advent of Neoclassicism in the second half of the eighteenth century.

At Versailles, the Rococo style of Louis XV was especially compatible with chinoiserie. Whole rooms, such as those at Chantilly, were painted with compositions in chinoiserie, and artists like Jean-Antoine Watteau brought consummate craftsmanship to the look. Thomas Chippendale, the chief advocate of Chinese style in England, was heavily influenced by patterns of latticework and decorative motifs expressed in Chinese architecture, absorbing them into his distinctive vocabulary. The craze even reached the American colonies, where Chinese wallpaper was as popular in colonial homes as it was in the grand palaces of Europe. In Philadelphia especially, chinoiserie had a pronounced effect upon colonial interiors.

In Europe, chinoiserie culminated in whole interiors being decorated in the style, most famously at the Petit Trianon in Versailles and the legendary apartments decorated by Madame de Pompadour, who remained faithful to chinoiserie

Early Chinese potters were believed to use magic to transform earth, fire and water into works of beauty and functionality. By the fourteenth century, ceramics were considered to be one of China's highest art forms, and *longquan* vessels like these were found in temples and palaces. A type of celadon, *longquan* was made throughout the Song dynasty, and was widely exported for centuries afterwards.

Although the Chinese had the technology and materials to make glass goblets, custom dictated that liquids were served in porcelain vessels decorated with elaborate, almost ceremonial, motifs. Wine cups like these were made in the palace workshops during the Kangxi reign. They were highly prized by French merchants, who dubbed them *famille rose* because of their tints of delicate pink.

throughout her life. King Adolf Fredrik of Sweden famously built an entire Chinese pavilion at Drottningholm Palace, near Stockholm, which he presented to his German-born wife, Queen Lovisa Ulrika, on her thirty-fourth birthday. The two-storey pavilion consists of an oval reception room, opening into drawing rooms on either side, which in turn open into galleries. Some of the most complete and perfect examples of chinoiserie interiors, the rooms are brilliant in colour and extravagantly mirrored. Wall paintings depict the mythical inhabitants of Cathay, idling away their time as they arrange flowers, play musical instruments and lie in dreamy reverie under parasols. In other parts of the pavilion, walls are panelled with the lacquered sections of Chinese screens, and delicately carved furniture is upholstered in embroidered silk. Walls are covered with Chinese wallpaper and woodwork trim is painted dark red to match, while every niche, shelf and alcove is filled with porcelain treasures. Not to be outdone, the queen's relations built chinoiserie pavilions across Germany with great speed, many of which survive today.

Chinoiserie, despite its Westernized shapes and decorations, remains an important part of China's own cultural history, where it also represents the continuation of a long tradition of manufacturing export goods. Over several millennia, Chinese traders had established workshops across the country to produce goods for exchange along the Silk Route. Long before China began trading with the West, Persian and Arabic merchants had commissioned its workshops and factories to manufacture wares specifically for export to Asia and the Middle East.

In the minds of Europeans, chinoiserie conjured up images of elaborately decorated Chinese homes rich in colours, textures and embroideries. To a large extent, Europeans believed that the exotic interiors they created were accurate replications of authentic Chinese interiors. In fact, the decorative arts made for export by the Chinese bore little resemblance to authentic decoration found in China. Little did the Europeans realize that merchants had encountered Ming styles years earlier, but judging them too austere for European tastes, focused on exporting the staples of tea and silk instead. As Guangzhou (Canton), for many years the sole point of commercial contact with the West, became more industrialized, European merchants commissioned elaborate objects for export just as the Persian and Arabic merchants had done along the Silk Route many centuries before.

Early in the Ming dynasty, the fourteenth-century missionary visitors to China who managed to penetrate the homes of rich merchants and high nobles were struck by their relative simplicity. Few decorative surfaces or soft furnishings were found, while simple but sophisticated paintings and hanging scrolls took the place of the wall murals and tapestries they were familiar with in Europe. Those were described in the sixteenth century, by the Augustinian friar, Juan Gonzalez de Mendoza, who wrote in awe of houses as large as entire European villages, but seemed unimpressed by their white walls, stone floors and wooden ceilings.

Prior to the Ming dynasty, Chinese interiors had been even simpler, resembling those prevalent in Japan today. As most activities took place at floor level, mats were used in place of chairs. Footwear was removed and seating was either directly on the floor or on low platforms covered with matting or textiles. The Japanese adopted the lifestyle of the Chinese during the Tang dynasty and conserved and adapted it for many centuries to follow.

Despite the seemingly austere shapes and undecorated surfaces of the Ming dynasty, architecture, furniture and home decoration reached their zenith during this period. Lines were clean and spare, with much emphasis placed on the lustre and grain of the wood itself. Every conceivable decorative detail was carefully considered, before being incorporated into a system so highly aestheticized that the scale and proportion of architecture determined the design not only of the furniture but also of the tiniest craft details. In a decorative context, Ming style can be loosely compared to the Puritan simplicity of England in the sixteenth and seventeenth centuries, which ended with the Restoration in 1660, when Charles II and his courtiers returned from Europe with a taste for opulence. Echoes of the Ming style can also be found in the Shaker style of nineteenth-century America.

The elegance of Ming style was achieved by a sophistication in materials, construction and design motifs that was expressed in architecture, furniture and ornamentation. Few foreign influences affected the style; from around 1450 Ming rulers pursued a policy of isolationism and forbade foreigners to enter the country, and this was continued for several centuries. Despite China's vast size, the principles of Ming design was practised throughout the country, uniting it in a style that amplified the esoteric principles of house design outlined by the ancients. Ming artisans reinterpreted the Chinese preference for living amidst elements from the natural world, articulating a system of balancing the natural with the artificial that continues today.

Following the collapse of the Ming dynasty in 1644, the understated tastes of the Han Chinese (the native Chinese ethnicity) slowly gave way to the exaggeratedly ornate style of the Manchu conquerors. The Manchu rulers displayed their power in expansive gowns and headdresses designed to reflect the very breadth of their magnificence, and decorated their homes with equal panache. During the Qing dynasty, established by the Manchus, arts and crafts seemed to be a part of the political agenda, driving Manchu tastes and values into the home itself. This was the antithesis of the classical Ming style, which was considered to be the height of Han Chinese sensibilities.

The Manchus introduced deep hues of red and yellow to the home interior, with accents of gold, turquoise, black and light green. Red became emblematic of the power and vibrancy of the Manchu reign, and still has these associations for the Chinese today. The Manchus were strictly Buddhist rather than Taoist or Confucian, and their tastes were influenced by temple decoration, whose bright colours had probably originally come from India centuries before as the teachings of the Buddha spread east. Qing decoration brings warmth to any interior, but with it comes the

The Manchu rulers of the Qing dynasty created some of the most opulent fashions ever worn in China, as seen on this Manchu bride of the late nineteenth century. Her outer robe was made to wear over a gown coloured in deep red and bright gold, probably with stiff cuffs styled in the shape of a horseshoe, and heavily ornamented with embroidery. The headdress, like her gown, would have been made in red and gold. Many of the Manchu elite dressed in this style every day.

struggle to keep the rest of the decor simple. Ironically, the word *qing* means 'clarity' or 'purity', which is at odds with the confusing styles and chaotic tastes that characterized the dynasty.

By the mid- to late nineteenth century, Chinese interiors had become brightly coloured and heavily ornamented, emulating European Baroque and Rococo styles. This is attributed to the relatively relaxed foreign policy of the Qing sovereigns; under their rule the West was able to explore China beyond the trading ports, and the occasional emissary was received in the capital. Many European courts presented gifts of furniture and textiles to the emperor, and these objects influenced the decor of the palace and the interiors of the nobility, trickling down to the homes of mandarins and merchants. Chinese furniture and screens became heavy, dark and carved; ceramics lost their refinement and appeared ornate and heavily embellished; curtains and drapes were made of thick velvet and richly embroidered; and lanterns became laden with medallions and red tassels.

In the mid-eighteenth century, at the height of the Qing period, the Emperor Qianlong decided to construct Yuanmingyuan, a complex of European palaces loosely based on Versailles. Vast Neoclassical pavilions, garden mazes and mechanical fountains, great marble arches, galleries and banquet halls all created in Beijing an image of 'Europeanoiserie' built astride Chinese-style parkland. The palaces themselves were seldom referred to in the West, but the magnificent gardens served as the inspiration for many of the beautiful chinoiserie gardens that were built throughout Europe in the eighteenth and nineteenth centuries.

The fall of the Qing dynasty in 1911 didn't end Qing style or chinoiserie; they spread further west as the Chinese emigrated to Europe and North America, where many Chinese homes and restaurants are decorated in pastiche versions of Qing style today. In China, the Qing treasures were shared with the people by opening palaces to the public and turning grand estates into public parks. To the Chinese, Qing seems a bit old-fashioned. Though the period began and ended in political turmoil, Qing will always seem tied to its Manchu heritage and Western chinoiserie. Ming styles are making a marked comeback, with many classical Ming shapes regarded as contemporary today. Qing and Ming styles came closer together when the Qing aesthetic gave way to Art Deco, creating streamlined shapes that recalled the elegance associated with Ming.

Often modern Chinese choose to return to the reverence for simplicity that characterized the Ming period, pushing excessive ornamentation aside and highlighting only essential elements and subtle colours. The recent resurgence of

The ceramics of the Tang dynasty were characterized by rich colours and bold patterns that today are mirrored in some of the abstract patterns created by contemporary ceramicists. Vibrant motifs like the one on this platter were created by mixing pieces of straw with the wet glaze, or dusting the piece with charcoal and ash before firing.

An indicator of status, dragons were associated with power and protection. This Qing dish is adorned with scrolling rims and wave motifs that recall the blue-and-white ceramics typical of the early Yuan dynasty. A plate of this design would have been used on formal or ritual occasions, given as a gift, or awarded to officials for services to the court.

Ming style shows how well these timelessly classic pieces work with modern trends. This type of minimalism not only involves negation, subtraction and purity, but also reduces the decorative process to the basic concepts of light, volume and mass. By eliminating all superfluous ornamentation, Ming designers were able to make features out of the home's interior proportions by contrasting strict symmetry with irregular shapes. For modern minimalists, the Ming style returns to the starting point of interior design to arrive at the essence of elegant style. But the possibilities for injecting Chinese style into the home are not simply limited to minimalism – the lavish ornamentation of the Qing period creates rich, exotic overtones that either transform an interior into a shrine of Oriental splendour or denote the decadence of an opium den.

In recent years the concept of Chinese design has been restricted to archaeological pieces in museums or those mass-produced, poor-quality wares branded with the ubiquitous 'Made in China' label. As twenty-first century China takes its next great leap forward, Chinese designers and manufacturers have started working from a point where they can adopt ancient principles and at the same time express contemporary, visionary attitudes that will redefine the historic notions of Chinese style. The teapot has, for example, been produced for over a thousand years while the rice bowl and the high-necked vase have been produced continuously for three thousand years. Compared with the West, where an object manufactured continuously for a mere fifty years is celebrated as a design classic, China has a rich sense of design history that is astounding and inspirational.

As the best and most appealing aspects of Chinese style and design are brought vividly to life in this book, the timeless elements of the Ming and Qing periods have been adapted for the contemporary interior along with the more exotic visions of some of the world's leading contemporary designers. *Chinese Style* is a fascinating journey through the Chinese interior itself, juxtaposing its rich, detailed history with bold new directions for the home. Organized in six practical sections, the book explores the vibrancy and equanimity that this seductive style can bring to the Western interior. Drawing inspiration from furniture, ceramics, textiles and artefacts, *Chinese Style* is a comprehensive study that examines the design principles behind Chinese architecture and space planning, the beauty of antiques and decorative arts, and the uses of traditional colours and motifs. As a practical guide to introducing elements of Chinese chic into the Western home, *Chinese Style* offers accessible ways to inject new inspiration into the interior, or completely rethink your living space in line with Chinese sensibilities. *Chinese Style* will appeal to anyone with an appreciation of pure form, innovative design, understated luxury or exotic decor.

ARCHITECTURE

建築

ARCHITECTURE

In China, architecture has been considered an extension of nature since ancient times. The wood and stone harvested from forests and quarries remained a part of the natural world even after they had been reborn as houses and temples. All buildings were regarded as an integral part of their surroundings, their placement influenced by their proximity to rivers, plains, mountains and the sea. The ancients believed that forces in the natural world held the secret to prosperity, longevity and happiness, and Chinese architecture became an essential part of a system advocating living in harmony with the environment and the earth. Philosophers believed that the presence of *qi*, or *chi*, meaning 'life energy', in the landscape would indicate the areas most fertile for agriculture and best sheltered from inclement weather. Their regard for these places determined where people would live, cultivate land, build temples and bury their dead. The belief in invisible forces generated a profound respect for all aspects of the physical world, gradually evolving into the concepts of yin and yang, feng shui, Taoism and the *Yijing* (the *I Ching*, or the 'Book of Changes'), which are still observed in modern times.

Feng shui translates as 'wind and water'. According to this philosophy our lives and destinies are closely interwoven by the workings of the universe and of nature. The invisible *qi* can be directed into a harmonious flowing energy that enhances the life force in our bodies, eliminating any element that may cause an imbalance. The aim of feng shui is to add balance to the surrounding environment so that harmonious energy fields prevail throughout. The ideal living space can be perfectly aligned with the cosmos, by bringing it in line with the polarities of north and south, symbolically linking it with heaven as well as earth.

Traditionally, the most auspicious places to dwell are found on flat terrain among hills or mountain ranges. The ancients searched far and wide to find the most powerful sites in the landscape, where houses and tombs could be built in close proximity to hills and rivers. While any house could be constructed to counteract unlucky forces, those built on hill plateaus with an open southerly view over a gentle river or stream were thought to be protected from the effects of negative *qi*. The proximity to flowing water would increase the flow of positive *qi* around the house, while the hills surrounding the site at the rear and sides would prevent it from flowing away too quickly.

Auspicious spots were usually associated with energy lines in the landscape, and whole cities would be erected on so-called 'dragon lines of *qi*'. Individual homes were planned in relation to sources of *qi* in the natural world, and also to those in the man-made landscape. The Chinese character for 'wall' and 'city' is one and the same; the massive walls built to fortify cities also served as a starting point for the symmetrical division of space in the north–south orientation. Homes throughout the land were built on a north–south axis, with the main part of the house positioned to face south, flanked by rooms of lesser importance on the east and west. Houses were typically enclosed by thick walls, resembling complexes of cloistered buildings separated by courtyards.

The formula for domestic architecture and its principal decorative features has changed very little over the last three thousand years. Large family homes often originated as modest dwellings with only a set of rooms surrounding a walled garden,

which grew in size as subsequent generations added more rooms and additional courtyards. The household often included groups of seven or eight families, or large clans sharing several interlocking dwellings. In ancient times tax relief was given to individual households, regardless of their size. The taxation laws were complex, and as they changed from taxing the household to taxing the married couple, clans moved apart, but several generations of the same family remained together – a tradition that continues today.

Despite their unpredicted expansion, homes of this type were well planned, with the space apportioned into four different areas: the formal reception rooms, the family's residence, the garden courtyard and the studio. Although vernacular Chinese architecture differed among its varied landscapes and many far-flung provinces, common to all was a careful balance between the practical needs of the household, the concept of ya, or elegance, and the designation of separate living spaces. By creating several very different environments under a single roof, the Chinese achieved varied surroundings in which the household could find beauty and serenity when they closed the doors on the outside world.

The basic structure of a traditional Ming house involved a network of timber columns that were interconnected by horizontal beams, supporting a curved, overhanging roof made of ceramic tiles. The columns rested on round stone plinths and rose in an unbroken line from the floor through to the open rafters. The upturned eaves were designed to direct rainfall away from the house, while also letting more light through to the rooms within. The roof tiles were angled to form gullies that channelled water over the eaves, with triangular drip tiles turning the flow of water into a curtain of raindrops.

Throughout the house, the height of the rooms extended to the eaves, where panels of fretwork buttressed the columns or lined the beams overhead. The soft tones of native hardwoods gradually deepened over the years to a warm brown, and the fragrance of the wood lingered in the interior for years. The rich natural pattern of woodgrain was highly regarded, and wood was treated as a decorative element in itself. Stone was held in the same esteem; marble, jade and amber were inset into the wall or mounted on it to highlight the beauty of the shapes contained in their grain. Floors were laid in terracotta, granite or other light-coloured stone, and sporadically covered with rugs made of cotton or wool. The natural colours created a sense of visual harmony, with the smoothness and cool colouring of the floor tiles enhancing the rich brown and red tones of the wood.

Window openings were spaced unevenly to counter the precise symmetry of the architectural supports, while the fretwork covering them was also designed to contain subtle differences to create variety within uniformity. The contrasts between open window frames and solid walls were seen as a juxtaposition of positive and negative shapes, providing a subtle representation of yin and yang. Windows overlooking a garden were sometimes cut into the shape of lanterns, flowers, moons or fans. Regarded as 'picture windows', they literally framed a carefully composed 'painting' of beautiful plants and flowers.

Page 19 Large Chinese homes almost always included a study or studio to which individuals could withdraw for some peace and quiet. Today Western architects recognize the value of such spaces, designating tranquil areas where the occupants can relax, and escape from the pressures of modern life. Latticework window shutters have always provided privacy, also filtering the sunlight and camouflaging urban scenery.

Above The Chinese often treat the view as part of a picture. Window openings are cut in a variety of shapes and configurations, framing the view of the plants in the garden beyond. They may also be fitted with geometrical fretwork or elaborate carvings, such as this silhouette with its poetic depictions of nature.

The Formal Rooms

Situated along a north–south axis, the house was traditionally built with the formal rooms to the south, so that they overlooked both the gate at the front of the house and the courtyard at the centre; the private rooms for the family were built on the other side of the courtyard, to the north. In the formal rooms, visitors were received, guests entertained and business transacted. The formality and status of these rooms were emphasized by the poetic names they were given. Titles like the 'Hall of Gathering Elegance' and the 'Hall of Ascending to the Clouds' were especially popular.

Depending on the wealth and status of the owners, the formal part of the house could be a large, single room, or several interconnecting rooms separated by screens or double doors. These rooms were usually rectangular in shape, divided by columns into several bays with banks of alcoves on either side. Latticework screens provided intimacy within the large rooms, creating an internal structure and dividing up the space. A screen was typically constructed to span the space between two columns, which supported it on either side. When placed directly in front of a doorway, screens were believed to ward off spirits, since the Chinese ghosts of legend cannot turn sharp corners. Ghosts cannot step over obstructions either, which is why the *menkan*, a raised wooden threshold, would be placed across each doorway.

Below left Latticework screens can be fitted from floor to ceiling to restructure a room, providing both privacy and a sense of scale without blocking the passage of light. Free-standing screens also make practical room dividers as they can be easily moved to redefine floor space and living areas, or create shadows and diffused lighting.
Opposite Traditional domestic architecture divided the Chinese home into four distinct living spaces: the formal rooms, the family's private residence, the courtyard garden and the studio or study. The private rooms for the family were where the children played and the family worked and slept, prepared food and carried out domestic chores.

Floor space was determined more by the positioning of screens than by the design and layout of the room. Because screens were treated as partition walls and were generally placed at right angles to the existing walls, they divided the floor space into rectangles, with the furniture arranged between them.

Although important pieces like armchairs and couch beds were usually placed in the centre of the room, secondary items such as straight-backed chairs and occasional tables usually lined the walls. This maximized the open spaces in the interior, allowing the eye to travel uninterrupted from wall to wall.

When family gatherings or social events were held, the furniture was pulled into the centre of the room, opening up space along the walls for people to move freely from one side of the room to another.

Opposite The main entrance to a Chinese home is often described as the front gate, which historically was wide enough for a sedan chair or carriage to enter. In China today this gate is usually replaced by a reinforced door, but some homes symbolically recreate it through latticework panels or elaborate door frames. Superstition dictated that *menkan*, raised wooden thresholds, were fitted to ward off spirits, since the Chinese ghosts of legend are not able to pass over obstructions. *Menkan* are a distant memory in modern China.

Above The shape and style of Ming tables often determined their function. Square tables were usually designated for game playing, flanked by matching stools or high-backed chairs. These armless 'official's chairs' are so called because the top of the backrest resembles the shape of the hat worn as part of the bureaucrat's uniform. The small, square pieces pictured here, however, were crafted in a uniquely multipurpose design; they were made to double as stools or occasional tables, or for use as steps to reach high places.

The streamlined elegance of Ming style resurfaced in the early twentieth century to influence Art Deco styles. The contours of this set of modern furniture mirror the graceful shapes of Ming style, while the upholstery recalls the signature crimson of the Qing dynasty. The fusion of gentle shapes and rich colours counters the angular architecture of this minimal twenty-first-century interior.

The balance and harmony achieved in Ming interiors were attributed to the precise symmetry followed in furniture placement. The alignment of the chairs shown here defines the different living areas of the room; they are an effective and unobtrusive means of dividing space.

The Family Residence

The residence was less formal in its arrangement of furniture and perhaps the cosiest part of the house. It contained the rooms where the family worked and slept, located at the rear of the house near the kitchen, or situated on the first floor where they were accessed via enclosed staircases. Long corridors running parallel to the formal rooms led from the entrance directly into the family rooms or the kitchen, allowing members of the household to bypass the main parts of the house as they came and went.

The kitchen stove – usually a mammoth brick or earthenware structure – was constructed by the house builders. Though stoves of this type are no longer built, many still survive and remain in use today. This type of stove had a chimney but bore little resemblance to a European fireplace or ceramic stove. It was stoked with wood or coal from underneath and cooking was done in pots and pans set into its oven-like alcoves.

Whether the home was humble or palatial, no more than one stove would ever be built, as the Chinese believe that the family who eats food prepared in the same stove is symbolically one unit. If two brothers decided to split their families apart and live separately, the ashes of the communal stove would be distributed between them to represent the division.

The stove was also the location of one of the most powerful household deities, the kitchen god, who watches over all family activities and reports annually to the heavenly emperor on their behaviour. His shrine – also shared with his wife and children – is built into the stove as a shelf on the chimney. Families burned incense and presented fragrant offerings in their attempts to placate this revered spirit. The main household shrine was usually situated in the formal rooms. Elaborately decorated with pictures of Buddhist deities and statues of the Buddha, it was also adorned with devotional objects. Flower vases, scented candles and porcelain bowls of fruit offerings fill the air with the fragrances of lemon, sweet basil, citronella, sandalwood and rosewood.

Despite China's temperate climate the winters can be severe, and the risks of using open fireplaces in a wooden house horrified the Chinese. Therefore, in the cooler seasons coals from the stove would be shovelled into metal braziers and placed throughout the house. The family insulated the rooms by hanging heavy, padded textiles over the doorways and window shutters, and around beds and sleeping areas. In the north of China, domestic architecture was characterized by substantial stoves and the large *kang* built in the family rooms, many of which are still in use today. Resembling a raised brick platform with a stove underneath, a *kang* can occupy a third of a room, and provides a place for sleeping, eating and relaxing in the winter months. Homes in the northern regions were often built with flat roofs to keep the warm air circulating in the living space rather than letting it escape to the rafters above.

The studio was a room, or a set of rooms, devoted to the practice of the visual arts. Writing, like painting, was considered an art form, and the calligrapher and painter worked seated at desks and tables rather than standing at easels. Typically located in a quiet part of the house, the studio was a place where members of the household could retreat in solitude. Here the scholar might write poetry, create flower arrangements, study the Confucian classics, or spend evenings gazing upon the moon in quiet contemplation.

Opposite Families surrounded themselves with stylized 'ancestor portraits', which were painted on scrolled parchment or silk and hung in places of honour. They were venerated by the family, who burned candles and incense to appease their spirits and invoke their continued benevolence and protection.

Page 30 Architectural features are sometimes the starting point for transforming a Western interior into a Chinese room. This fire surround recalls the Western trend for chinoiserie elements and creates a focal point around which other Chinese details have been added.

The sense of symmetry characteristic of Chinese interiors illustrates the ancient expression, 'All good things come in pairs'. The pairing of two pieces of furniture is considered auspicious. According to Chinese legend, placing two objects alongside each other creates a cosmic gateway though which invisible blessings can come. The Ming tables, chairs and benches give this contemporary study a tranquil feel.

Opposite and this page
Ming style easily lends itself to the most minimal modern living space. Featuring a few period pieces in a contemporary setting injects the flair of another era to create an artistic feel. This approach works best with smooth surfaces and subtle colours that allow antiques to stand out. Though the low table (below) is more than six hundred years old, its streamlined style seems just as contemporary as the modular furniture surrounding it. The dining table and benches (opposite) are also antique, their unadorned shapes adding a rustic element to the room.

The Courtyard

As well as being designated for the cultivation of plants, flowers and small trees, the courtyard served as an extension of the house. Either it was situated in the middle of the house, surrounded by rooms on all four sides, or it was enclosed by rooms on three sides and the high, whitewashed perimeter wall on the fourth side. Every house was defined by its surrounding wall, and to create a garden without enclosing it on all sides was almost unthinkable to the Chinese. The courtyards were paved with bricks or terracotta tiles. The eighteenth-century Emperor Qianlong started a vogue for bluish-grey terracotta tiles when he built his own garden courtyard in the Forbidden City in Beijing.

Water was the garden courtyard's main focus as well as its physical centre. Small ponds were dug in irregular shapes to create narrow coves that could be spanned by stone bridges – either arched or zigzag in shape – creating the illusion that water continued to flow into unseen parts of the landscape. The ponds were filled with lotus pods, lily pads and goldfish with bulging dragon eyes and ribbon-like tail fins. The murmuring sound of tiny waterfalls and winding rivulets of water flowing over pebbles and rocks filled the air, along with birdsong and the chirping of crickets. Children caught crickets in special cages to bring their rhythmic tones indoors for the adults to hear, or captured fireflies to use in lanterns as nightlights.

Water immediately brings to mind the principles of yin and yang so fundamental to Chinese architecture. In contrast to the inherent yang of the hard, dry stone, clay and timber used to construct the house, the water nourishing the core of the home brought yielding yin elements of softness, moisture and coolness. Its vitality nourished foliage around it and represented a continuation of the life force for the plants and the inhabitants. To the Chinese, water also signifies that which is pure and noble, and ultimately true to its nature, following its own path and seeking its own level.

Porches or pavilions were built in styles and proportions appropriate to the house, providing additional spaces for entertaining, relaxing or carrying out household tasks. Larger homes occasionally featured pavilions and pagodas in architectural styles that differentiated them from the main house, so as to create a trompe l'oeil effect that made the rest of the house virtually disappear from view. These areas were especially inviting in the summer months, where they would have been cooled by the water around them and the breezes passing through the latticework walls.

Those who did not venture into the garden could enjoy nature in the form of elegant *penjing*, or 'flowerpot landscapes', similar to the *bonsai* known in Japan. Held in the same artistic esteem as painting or poetry, these displays of miniature landscapes created for the interior were painstakingly detailed and true to nature. Proud gardeners might commission a replica of their own garden or a model of an area of outstanding natural beauty nearby. These were generally made specifically for each home, and great sensitivity was practised in choosing the colours, lines and textures of the plant material and the platter. Minute trees appeared to grow at the base of rocks grouped to resemble miniature mountains, transforming pebbles into boulders. Creating these table landscapes is by no means a lost art in China: they remain an area of both popular and scholarly interest and are found in homes, shop windows and botanical gardens.

The garden courtyard was the hub of the traditional Chinese house; it bridged the formal rooms and the private residence. The rooms adjacent to the courtyard were designed with doors and windows that opened onto it, inviting the fragrance of flowers and plants and the gentle sound of running water into the house. Guests were expected to admire the garden, and etiquette dictated that they be seated with a garden view, while the hosts would face in the direction of the front gate.

Yin & Yang

The active energy of yang and the passive energy of yin symbolically reverberates throughout the rest of the structure and into the interior itself. Balance is considered an important element in every aspect of the home, from the shape and location of rooms to the arrangement of furniture. Chinese architecture incorporates polarities of light and dark, soft and hard, rounded and angled. The circle is used to counter the triangle, and dark colours and shade are juxtaposed against sunlight and brightness: constant reminders that life should be lived in balance. This philosophy does not stand independently from other everyday customs of design and decoration, and is integrated into everyday life where it continues to play a role today.

The concepts of yin and yang imply both independence and interaction, their combinations symbolizing infinite change in nature as in life, all leading towards ultimate harmony in the universe. Both of these opposites are half-completed statements, awaiting unification with the other half. To the Chinese, balance is not stasis, but a controlled fluctuation of the extremes. In a spatial sense, this can be achieved by the combination of different elements that remain distinct from each other but ultimately blend into a harmonious whole.

This page and opposite The principles of yin and yang are fundamental to the Chinese interior. The positive elements of yang and the negative elements of yin are juxtaposed to create a sense of equilibrium: darkness is contrasted with light, solid forms are countered with soft textures, and rough surfaces are paired with smooth ones.

The materials used to build a traditional home were also perceived in terms of their characteristics. The strength of timber enabled it to support a heavy roof and tolerate harsh weather, and, with its unassuming beauty, provided an unfinished surface that could be beautifully ornamented. Such characteristics were metaphors for the upright character of the Confucian scholar, who was humble yet dared to uphold principles when challenged, and remained true to his spiritual nature despite worldly temptations, fashioning his character with few superficial influences.

Applied to the Western interior, the principles of yin and yang can also be used to create contrasting areas, or to design interiors that can be easily changed between contrasting moods. The relationship of darkness and light can be reversed using curtains, blinds, screens, candles and incense to change the room's mood in an instant. This system, so utterly simple in principle, provides the basis to experiment and vary surroundings into an ever-changing, multi-functional environment. To explore fully the many functions furniture can have, create contrasts and discover unexpected juxtapositions is to allow the interior to work its own magic.

The Ming aesthetic still has an impact on homes today, as modern minimalism and Eastern philosophies converge to shape contemporary interiors. The surfaces of this room reveal the beauty of line and form, and the effect of vibrant colour. The low Ming altar table juxtaposes the old with the new, the light with the dark and the smooth with the patinated.

Great sensitivity was shown in coordinating a room's elements with its architecture, and the furniture and ornaments were designed to occupy specific places in the interior. High-backed chairs were made to be positioned in the centre of the room, facing each other or grouped around square tables. Low-backed chairs were intended to be placed under windows, or against the walls. The chairs shown here bear the shape of the 'official's hat chairs' shown on pages 25 and 27, but are crafted in lighter wood and fitted with armrests.

LIVING

The fabrics, furnishings and decorated objects prized by the West may have created a rich mythology of ancient Cathay, but they provided little insight into the customs, rites and rituals which they represented in the Chinese household. The tradition of the extended family living under the same roof is one of the oldest in China. The eldest male was considered to be the head of the family, while the women of the household, as a rule, were expected to obey their father in youth, their husband in marriage, and their son in old age. When a woman married, she would move to her husband's home and would remain with his family throughout her life, often forbidden to remarry if her husband died before her.

Not only was the family unit bound through kinship, but it was also united materially and ethically. Traditionally, China's entire social system tended to be family-centred, rather than oriented towards religion or the political state. The family was the chief source of economic sustenance, security, education and recreation and was even the primary religious focus through ancestor worship. Most household activities were strictly segregated by sex. Men usually ran the family business or worked as civil bureaucrats, and presided over the household's religious ceremonies, education, books, artwork and gardening, while women supervised domestic activities, the sewing of clothes and the weaving of textiles. Daily life for women was lived in accordance with the maxim, 'A girl's first concern is to be virtuous, her second, industrious'.

居住 LIVING

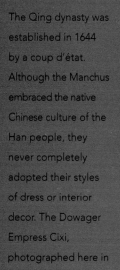

The most powerful female figure in China was Yehonala (1834–1908), the formidable Qing consort better known by the title of the Dowager Empress Cixi, whose strong control over the nation was unprecedented by any woman before her. Her lifetime spanned the gradual opening up of court life and signalled changes in status for all Chinese women. Criticized for her vanity, for her liberalism and ultimately for causing the collapse of the imperial regime, she circulated photographs of herself that were contrived to remind her subjects that reforms were taking shape at every level of Chinese society. Cixi famously composed her own photographic portraits, sometimes posing for the camera without wearing formal outer robes, in a breathtaking breach of protocol.

Historically, Chinese society was divided into four classes – mandarins (officials), peasants, artisans and merchants – and respected in that order. Though all aspired to serve the government in an official capacity, most of the population were resigned to humbler lifestyles. The Chinese elite were taught to idolize the humbler members of society. Following the example set by the renowned poet, Tao Qian (365–427), who abandoned the city for a home in the countryside, numerous urban scholars romanticized in poetry and literature the rustic lifestyle of provincial villagers.

The ancient Chinese applied the same intensity to building an environment for the afterlife as they did to creating their living spaces. They believed that life continued in the same form after death, so the dead should be as well equipped as the living. Tombs were constructed below ground, sumptuously equipped with all the furniture, utensils and clothing necessary for daily life. Buildings above ground were considered places provided for and protected by the ancestors for their living descendants – as long as they continued to respect and care for the well-being of the dead.

The Qing dynasty was established in 1644 by a coup d'état. Although the Manchus embraced the native Chinese culture of the Han people, they never completely adopted their styles of dress or interior decor. The Dowager Empress Cixi, photographed here in an opulent Qing interior at the turn of the twentieth century, wears traditional court robes and a distinctive Manchu headdress. Fashion and interior design were inextricably linked – both were designed to express the magnificence of the Manchu empire.

Throughout their long history, the Chinese have always placed great faith in the power of magic symbols. Every occasion has its symbolic emblems and rituals, from school ceremonies and religious observances to the birth, marriage and death of the ordinary

Symbols

citizen. The references are religious, superstitious or mythological, be they depictions of natural phenomena such as clouds, mist and rolling waves, or a zoology of wild animals. Birds are bestowed with moral and symbolic qualities: orioles represent the sun, the mandarin duck is associated with fidelity, while the magpie is a traditional symbol of luck. Dragons and other mythological beasts, lotus blossoms and chrysanthemums all remind the Chinese of an invisible world.

Each written Chinese character is pronounced as a single syllable, making the Chinese language rich in homophones, or words that have the same sound but different meanings. For example, *fu*, the Chinese word for bat, has the same sound as the term for good fortune, hence an image of the bat symbolized the word. As an image it was immediately recognizable by those who couldn't read or write, and such visual puns play an essential role in the choice of symbols for decoration.

Stoves are often decorated with images of fish because *yu*, the Chinese word for fish, is a homophone for the word meaning plentiful, and the family hope that their food supply will always be abundant. Many motifs result from the symbolic meanings given to words that have the same pronunciation as certain ambitions or blessings, giving birds and animals an important role in the visual language of decoration.

The twelve animals of the zodiac – rat, ox, tiger, hare, dragon, snake, horse, sheep, monkey, rooster, dog and boar – represent the characters of humans born under their sign and the basis of predictions for the future. In the astrological chart, the animals are paired with twelve 'earthly branches' in a system that combines them with ten 'heavenly stems' to form a cycle of sixty. The system is commonly used today as a way of marking time, identifying compatibility between individuals and divining the future. These signs are best known in the West among those interested in Chinese astrology, divination and the occult aspects of Chinese philosophies.

Symbols have high aesthetic and decorative value as well as symbolic meaning. Although a mantis (above left) sometimes represented cruelty, its presence in a motif also symbolized mystery. Birds (above centre) served as family emblems in ancient China and are often associated with allegorical folk tales. A river crab (above right) is a symbol of fertility. The dragon (opposite) rules over all other mythical creatures, but does not have the fierce reputation of its European counterparts. It is also an indicator of imperial rank.

The ancient Chinese delighted in natural forms, preferring motifs featuring flora, fauna (including mythological beasts), the changing seasons and landscape. Images of dragons range in shape and style from heavy, bulbous and rigid to the lithe and serpentine creatures shown here (above left). Sprays of wintersweet (above centre) remain as popular in modern fashion as they were on ancient robes. This bat (above right) flies among scrolling clouds set against a night sky. Scrolling clouds (right) were associated with deities, foretelling their arrival. The ubiquitous longevity symbol (left) was often considered a talisman to confer long life on the wearer. As well as appearing on textiles, it featured on ceramics and cloisonné, and on furniture during the Qing dynasty, when it was widely used.

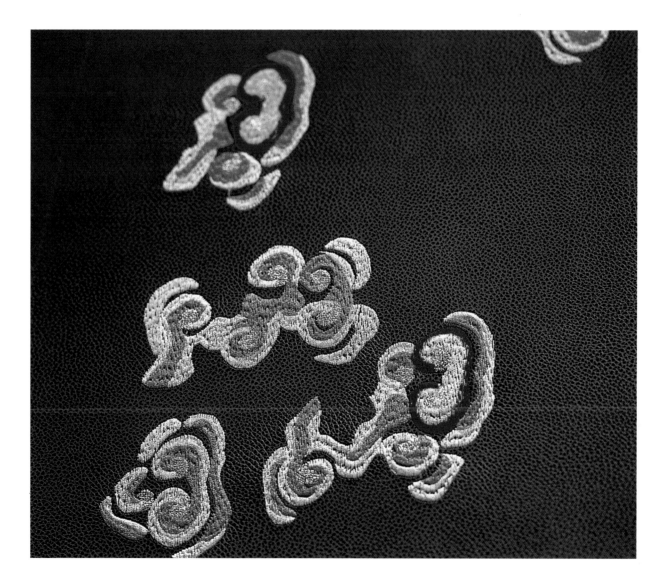

Festivals

The ancient Qing Ming Festival exemplifies the fundamental belief systems of the Chinese people. For thousands of years Chinese society has been organized on lines of respect for elders rather than the recognition of individual rights. Observance of respect to ancestors is an integral part of this system, and is a natural extension of the respect paid to living people who are older than oneself. It is the obligation of the young to show respect to their elders, and equally, the responsibility of the aged to teach these values to the young. Although the festival has a focus on remembering the dead, it is very much about the living family.

Qing Ming, meaning 'Clear and Bright', comes at the start of spring, when flowers are newly blossoming and the days are longer and brighter. In the Chinese lunar calendar, it is observed on the fourteenth day of the second month – in early April. Qing Ming is also associated with decorating graves and paying respect to the dead, which traditionally included preparing food offerings and burning goods in order to convey them to ancestors in heaven. Today, the living family enjoys the food, and the burnt offerings are made out of paper. Packets of paper clothing can be bought in Hong Kong and China to burn for the dead, sending them contemporary fashions to wear in the afterlife. The Chinese burn 'Bank of Hell' notes at the same time to distract any evil spirits attempting to intercept the goods; while the evil spirits are chasing the Bank of Hell money, the valuable goods pass safely to the dead.

Ever since the Xia dynasty, around four thousand years ago, the first day of the first moon in the lunar calendar has been a cause for celebration. New Year carnivals offer lantern and flower displays, lion dances, firecrackers and dragon processions. The celebrations – in early February – sometimes continue for an entire week, with preparations beginning weeks beforehand. The house is cleaned from top to bottom and decorated with fragrant fruits and flowers, and branches of pussy willow, plum or persimmon. The characters for health, wealth, longevity and good fortune are written on red paper in black or gold ink, then stuck to walls throughout the house.

Perhaps the most popular of all Chinese festivals, the New Year is regarded as an important family holiday. On New Year's Eve (the last day of the twelfth moon in the Chinese lunar calendar) the family gathers for a sumptuous meal, where everyone is careful not to drop their chopsticks, which could bring bad luck. The last baths of the year are taken to wash away all old luck, then everyone dresses in a new outfit to greet the year ahead. The entire family embarks on ritual 'New Year Visiting', when friends and relations greet each other and exchange good wishes. Known as the 'eight treasures', boxes of sweets, dried fruits, savoury nuts and seeds are prepared as snacks for visiting guests. It is also traditional to eat melon seeds to bring luck in the year ahead.

New Year's Day can start with children receiving from their parents their first red envelopes containing packets of 'lucky money'. Throughout the coming days friends and relatives give children more red envelopes – all to be immediately saved in a piggybank and increased throughout the year. No scissors or knives can be used on New Year's Day in case they 'cut short' the good luck that the New Year just brought in, so food is prepared the day before. Nothing can be washed all day either, to prevent the new luck from being rinsed away.

The Lantern Festival has been held for thousands of years. Today people still gather at dusk for the festival and fill the streets, carrying glowing lanterns and studying the sky overhead for the first signs of fireworks. Many families hang red lanterns over their doorways as their ancestors did, but chemical glow-sticks and mini-torches replace precarious flames. The lantern shown here is a modern reproduction of a traditional design.

The Lantern Festival falls on the fifteenth day of the first month in the Chinese lunar calendar, usually at the end of February. The exact origins of the tradition are unknown, but it may have evolved out of celebrations for the lengthening daylight that followed closely on from the New Year. Legends recall a Han dynasty emperor who ordered displays of light on the fifteenth night of the first lunar month to pay homage to Buddha, and Buddhists carried lanterns on this night to pay their respects. The festival itself takes its name from the Tang dynasty custom of hanging out lanterns on the night of the first full moon of the lunar year and lighting them nightly for several weeks afterwards.

The festival once lasted for forty-five days, but was gradually shortened to one week, then five days, and then three. Today, lanterns continue to be hung outside and throughout the house, and carried through the streets by children. The event is also famous for the moon-shaped rice flour dumplings filled with a variety of sweet fillings, popularly known as *yuanxiao* (literally 'round and little', like their shape), which is another name for the festival. Cities throughout China, Hong Kong and Taiwan hold elaborate festivals and huge lantern displays; coloured lanterns are strung together to form a shimmering lantern 'wall', and traditional dances are performed by dancers wearing costumes that glitter and sparkle in the light.

Few occasions are more joyous to the Chinese than a wedding. It is immediately distinguishable from other festivities, because almost everything relating to it is coloured red. Deep shades of scarlet, rich crimson, maroon and dark pink colour banners, lanterns, table coverings and garments. Traditionally, even the bride wears red, and the couple spend the wedding night sleeping in red linen. The 'double happiness' character (see page 169) – the symbol for marital bliss – originated in the Song dynasty, when a legendary scholar and statesman was a student awaiting his examination results. They arrived on his wedding day, with the news that his high score would almost certainly attract an imperial post. He expressed his delight by writing the character for happiness twice and joining them together as an expression of the double joy he experienced.

From this comes the Chinese saying, 'All good things come in pairs'. It is considered auspicious to put two chairs together or place two matching tables in a room. Portraits and scrolls are hung in pairs, while even lanterns are paired and potted plants placed side by side. A dragon and a phoenix are a mythical pair that represent the coupling of male and female virtues – the heavenly pairing of yin and yang energies. In Chinese eyes, placing two objects alongside each other creates a cosmic opening, a symbolic doorway though which invisible blessings can come.

On the wedding day, the groom calls for the bride at her home, and takes her to the wedding. The bride's friends demand 'lucky door money' before they allow the groom to collect her. The groom then counts the money aloud in denominations of nine, because the words *jiu* in Mandarin and *gao* in Cantonese, both meaning nine, are homophones for 'everlasting'. Whether the money adds up to ninety-nine pence or ninety-nine pounds is irrelevant – the ritual lends a witty modern twist to the ancient custom of the groom declaring an everlasting commitment to the bride and her family before the wedding. After the wedding, the food, gifts and decorations at the banquet feature in pairs, and the table, utensils and dishes are all coloured in shades of red.

Pages 50 & 51 The first day of the first moon in the lunar calendar was recognized as the official start of the Chinese calendar year, and a cause for celebration. Traditionally, the interior would be decorated with symbols of health, wealth, longevity and good fortune, but modern households may hang only paper lanterns, their glowing orbs mimicking the shimmer of moonlight. *Opposite* Dragon decorations can recall the festive spirit of the Chinese New Year. Origami dragons are easily refolded and stored, and they take seconds to hang up and create a festive mood. Paper dragons and dragon masks originated as an art form, requiring the combined skills of painters and sculptors to create their menacing faces and other-worldly bodies.

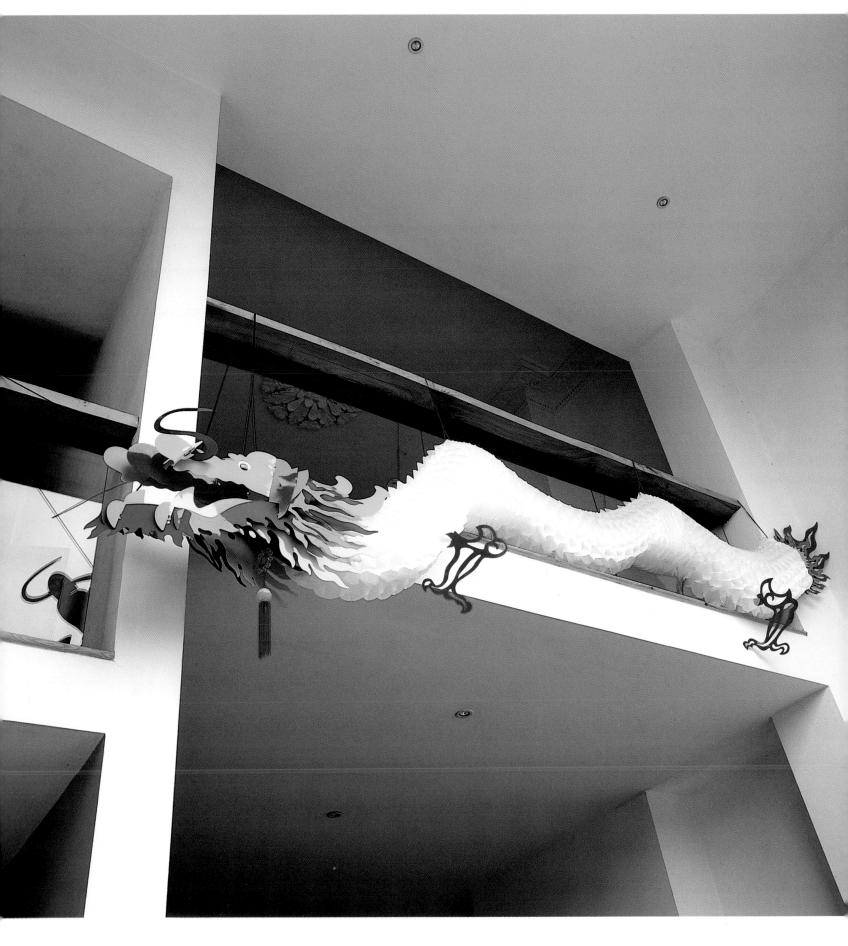

This page Supported here by a pair of Ming stands, the hanging lanterns appear as festive when placed on a table as they do suspended from the ceiling.

Opposite These crimson bed clothes are reminiscent of a Chinese marital bed. Tradition dictated that newlywed couples spent their first nights together in a bed swathed in red fabrics.

Eating

Living together and often working together, the family would also be united at mealtimes, religious ceremonies and festivals. Dining tables could be built to seat a family of ten or twelve; they were usually round, and of a size that would allow those seated to reach comfortably the dishes placed at the table's centre. Stools were universally used at dining tables, with only the aged seated at chairs. Traditionally, it was not unusual for the overall family unit to number well into the twenties or thirties – large households had to set up several tables at mealtime to accommodate the entire household. This is still the custom today, though families are much smaller now or live apart. Even at formal gatherings or festival dinners, groupings of smaller tables are customary rather than the long banquet tables used at formal dinners in the West.

Though meal presentation is a very important part of Chinese culture, there are fewer rules of etiquette to observe. The table setting has less importance than in the West – the placement of dishes and eating utensils is less formal. The Chinese begin the meal in order of seniority, with each diner beginning only after the older generations have started. Individual place settings include a rice bowl, a saucer, a pair of chopsticks and a flat-bottomed soup spoon, with rests for chopsticks and spoons placed alongside the rice bowl. Typically these are crafted in white porcelain decorated with coloured motifs and symbols conveying luck, long life and good fortune.

Below The Chinese have long preferred chopsticks to knives and forks, which they associate more with weapons and violence than with mealtime. Spoons (below centre) with 'lucky' symbols and spines crafted to mimic the segments of a bamboo tree were made for export in the Qing dynasty.

雲中彩鳳啣五色

Contemporary Chinese tableware combines ceramics, wood and lacquer to create modern displays based on historic designs. Platters crafted from bamboo are popular in the West for their stylish shapes as well as their antibacterial properties. Set on lacquerware flats, they inject a note of rustic elegance into a contemporary table setting, harmonizing with the altar scroll in the background.

Left Large, round tables are traditionally used at family mealtimes. Although rectilinear Western-style tables are becoming popular in the modern Chinese household, stools, rather than chairs, are likely to be used with them. Today's versions are made from metal with padded seats and swivel bases to suit contemporary sectional tables. All of the pieces shown here can be easily dismantled between dinner parties.

Opposite The hardwoods chosen for table tops are characterized by their fine grains and beautiful markings, which are left untreated, but are polished to a high sheen. This table was cut as individual quarters. Two of the quarters were cut on the cross grain and the other two on the lengthwise grain. When the segments are joined together into a circle, their grains create a contrasting pattern.

Chopsticks are thought to reflect the elegance and moderation encouraged in the teachings of Confucius. But there are superstitions associated with chopsticks, too. Finding an uneven pair at your table setting is believed to portend a missed boat, plane or train, or the arrival of a loved one. Dropping chopsticks is said to inevitably bring bad luck, while crossing chopsticks is strictly forbidden – unless done by a *dianxin* (dim sum) waiter to show that the bill has been paid. At the end of the meal, chopsticks should be balanced horizontally across the rim of the bowl or laid on the table beside the dish.

Beverages are not always served at mealtimes by the Chinese. Tea is drunk throughout the day, but with meals clear soup is usually the only liquid provided. When the Chinese are gathered together to drink tea, they are careful to ensure that the spout of the teapot is not pointing towards anyone, but is turned away from the table, preferably in a lucky direction.

This page Individual place settings can include a rice bowl and plates in varied sizes and colours. Eating utensils can be placed alongside the dishes, or poised on ceramic rests. Undecorated white porcelain makes an elegant statement, while pieces decorated with motifs and symbols will lend exotic overtones to any cuisine.

Opposite Tableware was often crafted from wood in regions where there was no local clay or kilns. Wooden dishes were painted with vernacular motifs and auspicious symbols, or lacquered to create a durable finish. Nutshells, seashells, horns and even animal bones were transformed into simple eating utensils and serving spoons.

Tea

According to Tang scholars, one of the best ways to delight in the garden was to take tea there. Tea symbolized an earthly purity that united man and nature. Culled from tender shoots that were painstakingly harvested and carefully steeped in hot water, tea was seen as the essence of nature itself – a distillation of the combined elements of the garden. Fragrant teas were made from infusions of lemongrass, geranium, maté or sweet basil. Teas from jasmine flowers and rose petals were highly treasured, but their rich flavours had to be drunk sparingly. Enjoyed as much for their taste as their aromatic properties, herbal teas were also taken as a tonic for good health, digestion and balance of energy. Believing tea to purified by the earth, the Chinese reasoned that its flavour should be treasured in small amounts.

The custom of drinking tea was part of a sophisticated spiritual and scholarly life, presided over by a benign 'tea art' spirit who belonged to the fairies of nature. As a rule, tea would be served in small terracotta teapots, since the full aromas and flavours of the tea were thought to disappear in a large one. The teapots were almost always white – at least on the inner surface – so that the tea drinker could fully appreciate its colour and tone. This tradition was passed down from the the sixteenth-century Ming court, which stipulated that the sensations enjoyed by the tea drinker should be warm and mellow, just like the hospitality offered in a Chinese home.

Below left Because tea was consumed in larger quantities in the West (the Chinese tended to sip it), Chinese craftsmen created teapots large enough to serve several guests.

Page 64 Tea is harvested from young, tender leaves, which are roasted and fermented, turning the dark green leaves reddish-brown. Here, tea leaves have been ground and pressed into decorative moulds to create the 'tea bricks' that make loose tea easier to pack and ship.

Page 65 The ancients identified seven basic daily necessities of life: fuel, rice, oil, salt, soy sauce, vinegar and tea. The custom of drinking tea, though not an elaborate ceremony as in Japan, continues to be an indispensable part of almost every social activity. This form of teapot emerged during the Tang dynasty.

There was a constant dialogue between the interior of the Chinese home and the courtyard. Flowers and plants entered the rooms, and the household furniture was sometimes placed outside. Plants and flowers were considered to be a necessary com-

Flowers & Plants

ponent of the interior, bringing nature indoors. Fragrant plants, especially summer orchids, were grown in ceramic pots placed on hardwood tables or on cane stands. *Hangchou*, the beguiling plant stands made from lacquered rootstock, provided elegant supports for the plant pots while suggesting that a web of intertwining roots emanated from underneath their base to the floor.

Flower arranging has for centuries been one of the traditional accomplishments of the scholarly class, and there have been many texts published on the subject. Scholars have written at length of the pleasures that can be derived from arranging rocks, flowers and potted orchids. The sensibilities that govern the Chinese interior also direct floral arrangements: trueness to nature, organic structure, rhythmic vitality and expressiveness. Two or three kinds of flowers can feature in each arrangement, provided that they are 'compatible'. Each and every flower has a symbolic association, directing which types of flowers should be grouped together or kept separate. For example, sprays of wintersweet and bamboo can appear together, both being symbols of winter hardiness. A peony, representing opulence and luxury, should never be placed alongside a pine bough, a symbol of austerity and fortitude.

Every flower, branch and leaf should be counted to ensure irregularity; an odd number is preferable since it is meant to convey the dynamic irregularity of the life force itself. Unopened buds should always be included among flowers in bloom, to celebrate life's continuing journey. The colours of the plants should coordinate with the colour of the container, and appear to spill naturally out of it. Arrangements following these principles were recorded in innumerable paintings from the Song dynasty onwards, the arrangements being positioned throughout the house on tables, stands and the shrine. The Chinese never have had anything as formal as the niche in the Japanese home, within which flower arrangements were meant to be placed; the placement of flowers within the Chinese home is much more fluid.

Below, far left Bamboo grows in a variety of sizes and grains, ranging from trees of immense proportions to lanky, weed-like sprigs.

Below left A hardy branch of cherry blossom against wallpaper.

Opposite As they prepare for the beginning of each festival, the Chinese fill their houses with vases of flowers and foliage. New Year decorations include branches of pussy willow, plum or persimmon, while the Qing Ming Festival celebrates the start of spring with newly blossoming flowers. Year round, the household shrine is adorned with fragrant flowers or bowls of fruit, bamboo shoots or budding plants.

Page 68 The calendar girls of the 1920s and 1930s were icons of style, introducing Chinese women to Westernized fashions, jewellery and hairstyles. Captured in a demure pose, this Shanghai lady cradles a stem of pussy willow, probably heralding the New Year or spring.

Page 69 Displays of flowers in the home have always provided more than just decoration; they inject a note of vitality into the interior and symbolize the life force itself. All flowers and plants are believed to radiate soothing *qi*, counterbalancing the robust energy of the dense stone and heavy timber used to construct traditional Chinese houses.

Wallpaper

The first Chinese wallpaper to reach Europe is thought to have arrived in the 1690s, and wallpaper maintained its popularity throughout the Georgian period. These papers were usually displayed as hanging scrolls in drawing rooms or as paper panels mounted onto screens. As chinoiserie became increasingly fashionable in Europe, many individual 'Chinese rooms' were decorated with imported wallpaper that was pasted directly onto the walls.

Wallpaper in China originated as a product of Ming austerity. Light-coloured paper was applied to mask the rough textures of stone or brick walls, and left undecorated. The paper was sometimes 'whitewashed' using the same technique of brush and paint as was used for decorating screens and scrolls. Wallpaper was never cut from rolls as it is today; it was constructed as panels that were pasted together in a patchwork of overlapping sheets.

Early eighteenth-century chinoiserie wallpaper was hand-painted with scenes or motifs before it left China, often illustrating brooding mandarins or resplendent ladies in elegant robes against a background of exotic flowers and mythological animals. A nickname for these was 'Long Elizas' – an anglicization of Lange Lijzen, the Dutch term for the willowy female figures on eighteenth-century Kangxi ceramics. Wallpaper told stories of mystery and charm, of a fairy-tale world among palaces, pagodas, fiery dragons and scrolling clouds. While these large-scale images would never have appeared in the interiors of the Chinese, they illustrated perfectly the eighteenth-century European fascination with Cathay.

Wallpaper was painted by the same method as was used to tint silk for furnishings, with the background washed in a single colour first; the preliminary outlining and final metallic highlighting indicate that the wallpapers and silks were probably painted in the same workshops. Most surviving examples show a mixture of Chinese mythological characters and hunting scenes. These were more to the tastes of Europeans than Chinese, especially since the Chinese had invented wallpaper to give rooms a smooth, uniform white surface rather than a decorative finish.

In the West in recent years, the return to pristine white walls or raw plaster meant that wallpaper was relegated to the margins of interior design. As wallpaper made a comeback with a wave of 1970s graphic motifs and pop art renderings for retro interiors, these were countered by authentic Chinese motifs and chinoiserie floral prints, which provided a soft backdrop for minimal styles. Ottilie Stevenson's chinoiserie range was inspired by a swatch of Chinese silk found in a Paris flea market, while the beautiful silk wallpaper designed by De Gournay recalls the elegant bird-and-flower motifs adorning paintings from earlier dynasties.

Most of the original chinoiserie motifs have been repeated over the years, copied again and again by successive waves of wallpaper and furnishing fabric manufacturers. This is why, unlike the ranges of popular prints that change with every new design wave, these motifs connect the contemporary era with the traditions established in the workshops of Canton three centuries ago. The impact that wallpaper has had on interiors has made it more popular than any other Chinese decorative export, maintaining a presence in Western interior design for centuries.

Though popular today, bird-and-flower motifs continue a painting tradition dating back several thousand years. As early interests in horticulture and botany evolved, the Chinese painted birds and flowers in great detail to record and catalogue native flora and fauna. In the eighteenth and nineteenth centuries, Western botanists collected these beautiful renderings for study, but the delicate beauty of their colours and forms was associated more with fine art than science, and Western designers appropriated their motifs for textiles and wallpaper, silk screens and ceramics.

Top left A simple leaf can capture the essence of a plant, as these feathery renderings illustrate. Their abstract shapes provide a timeless backdrop for antique textiles and furniture, or modern classics. *Bottom left* Wallpaper specialists such as De Gournay design large-scale representations of exotic landscapes to create the effect of a hand-painted mural. *Opposite* Reversing proportions is an eye-catching and effective device, overturning traditional ideas of scale and symmetry. As the wallpaper magnifies their foliage, these tropical plants become an overgrowth of elegant flora.

Left Geometry played an important role in the decorative arts of the Qing dynasty, when many classical motifs from previous eras were revived and executed in gold leaf against rich hues of red, green and blue. *Opposite* Birds and flowers have always had high aesthetic and decorative value in China. As they became popular in Europe in the eighteenth and nineteenth centuries, the painting studios in China adopted assembly-line methods to keep pace with demand. These chinoiserie styles were gradually developed to complement Western designs; the blend of styles and periods here captures the spirit of chinoiserie at its zenith.

Lighting

East or West, in every culture lighting is a powerful medium, one that highlights and defines the interior and creates both an overall ambience and an instant focal point. Throughout China's long history, lanterns have been an important decorative tradition, featuring in festivals and ceremonies as well as in homes, temples and palaces. They are traditionally made with frames that form a secure base when they are placed on a flat surface, or maintain their shape when hung overhead. Square, oblong or rectangular in shape, lanterns are made from paper or silk stretched around the frame to diffuse the light, and also to deflect the wind if hung outdoors. Circular lanterns were created to be hung overhead, their glowing orbs romantically viewed as representations of the moon.

Paper and cloth lanterns also have ceremonial associations in China. Red lanterns denote festivities of some sort, be it a wedding, a holiday or New Year, and usually have messages of good will written across them in black calligraphy. These decorate the front door and the interior during the celebration. Strung together in a single line, they are draped vertically along a wall or zigzagged across the centre of the room. Sometimes big lanterns are grouped in twos and threes and hung in varying lengths, with long red tassels dangling from each one's base. Traditionally paper lanterns were round or square, but today they can be shaped like hares, birds or dragons to symbolize the auspicious sentiments associated with these creatures.

Table lanterns can be made from glass, bamboo or metal wire, and covered with shades made from paper or silk. Unlike the orb shapes created from paper and silk, glass lanterns are usually square or multi-sided, with bamboo or copper ribs forming the structure of the frame. The panes of glass are often etched with motifs or inscribed with the symbols representing love, peace, joy or harmony, which would also be drawn on the fabric of a silk shade. The candle or light bulb inside is accessed by a hinged door on the side or by a top that can be removed altogether. Chinoiserie table lamps were cast in porcelain and painted in colourful motifs. Symbols were cut into the surface to provide perforations from which soft light could emanate.

Tall lanterns generally mirror the design of table lamps but are secured to a high base or tripod. During the Qing period these bases were elaborately decorated and often richly lacquered. Carved brackets joined the legs and the lantern's base to the stem, but could be detached so they could also be hung from the ceiling. Overhead lanterns were often the most richly detailed, providing the room with a magnificent central feature that even the Qing connoisseur might have considered over the top. Composed of several tiered layers varying in size, their frames were usually octagonal or heptagonal, descending from the largest at the top to the smallest at the bottom. The edges were elaborately ornamented with Baroque-like trim, or supported carvings of dragons and other-worldly creatures poised to frighten away spirits from every direction.

Today there are many more lighting methods available. Even though candles have been unromantically replaced with electric bulbs, Chinese shades still cast dramatic shadows and diffuse light to gently illuminate a room. Despite the fact that their origins are medieval, the simplicity of round paper shades gives them a modern feel. Qing-style lanterns lend an air of fun to any room, if not taking it over altogether.

The rectangular planes of this contemporary lighting display mirror the silhouette of a piece created by an earlier master. Lu Ban, China's legendary fourth-century BC furniture craftsman, designed simple shapes that have been in production ever since. The precise angles and contours used to construct the base and surface of this Ming altar table are attributed to Lu Ban, who set the tone for balance and elegance many centuries earlier. The illuminated walls were designed to evoke the tones of the deep blue visible in the misty landscapes of north China.

This Qing-style lantern combines Manchu ornamentation with superstition. Each paper panel is elaborately trimmed with ornate fretwork and supported by dragons and mythical creatures. Tassels, lucky charms and auspicious characters frighten away any spirits unlucky enough to venture in.

This light was made
from the appliquéd
cuff of an opera
costume. Antique
textile fragments are
often recycled as
lampshades, blinds,
valances and curtain
tie-backs, or framed
as works of art.

Left Paper lanterns are colourful and fun, easy to install and inexpensive to buy. These lanterns were initially strung up as party decorations, but have been left in place to create a festive atmosphere every day.

Opposite Late Qing craftsmen achieved beautifully shaped lanterns made from contoured brackets and sculpted stems, often intricately carved and richly lacquered. This shade recalls the shape of a lotus pod; its brackets and base represent the stem and roots that anchor the lotus to the pond bed beneath it.

Pages 82 & 83 Silk lampshades were traditionally made in rounded shapes to resemble the glow of the moon, as this beautiful light illustrates (left). Square and rectangular shades were not uncommon, but the Chinese regarded them as more functional than decorative. The soft lighting in this contemporary setting (right) updates these principles with a contemporary look, by combining angular shapes to create pillars, overhead lighting and discreet uplighters, concealed behind silk shades to diffuse their glow.

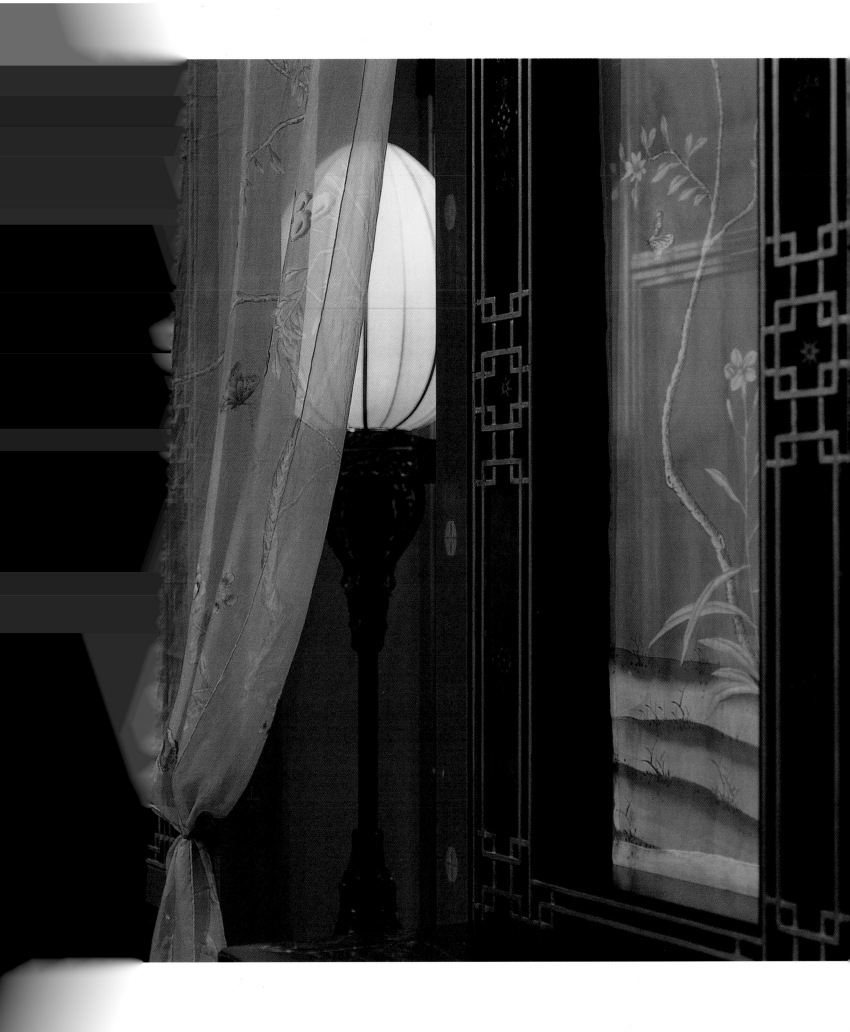

Colour

For a long period in Chinese history colour, especially bright colour, was not an important element of the interior. However, although plain whitewashed walls and natural finishes were celebrated throughout the Ming dynasty, colour was not completely absent. Cinnabar, a volcanic mineral that provided the pigments used to tint lacquers in the distinctive 'Chinese red', was also used to colour boxes, furniture and ornaments in a range of rich hues. Variegated porcelain pieces, flowering plants and arrangements of figurines made from jade, amber, lapis lazuli and other semi-precious stones were alternative sources of vibrant colours throughout the home.

Under the Manchu rulers of the Qing dynasty the Chinese developed a taste for more colourful and exuberant objects and motifs. The trend for elaborate decoration that persisted throughout the Qing dynasty brought dramatic hues of red, gold, turquoise and yellow to the home interior. Though the colour red was especially emblematic of the Manchu reign, it has also symbolized happiness for much of China's history, before and after the Qing dynasty, and still has these associations to the Chinese today. As the Qing dynasty unfolded, the interiors of the late eighteenth and nineteenth centuries became brightly coloured and heavily ornamented, emulating European Baroque and Rococo styles.

Colour symbolism has always been extremely important to the Chinese. In the early dynasties five basic colours were identified and assigned to represent the four cardinal directions of north, south, east and west, plus the central axis between them. They were also correlated with the five elements of water, fire, wood, metal and earth. Theories of yin and yang also provided a basis for the properties of colour, with black symbolizing yin, or the female, the moon, water, winter and rejuvenation. Black is also the colour of the north according to the traditional Chinese cardinal points, and it evokes the will to delve deeper within oneself or gain wisdom. The colour red represents yang, or the male, the sun, fire, summer and activity. Red also corresponds to the south and represents the desire to express oneself outwardly.

Yellow symbolizes the earth and the centre, but was also the imperial colour reserved for the emperor, the empress and the dowager empress. Because the earth has a responsibility to sustain mankind, yellow invokes the function of primary sustenance and nutrition, and therefore the emperor's role was to protect and nourish his people. The Chinese described their land as the 'yellow earth'. They also regard the earth as the centre of all their bounty: metals are extracted from the earth's mines and water flows from its wells. The plants they eat sprout from the earth, and it is also where fire breaks out.

The colour green, which relates to the east, is also the colour of the world of plants and nourishment, and a symbol for springtime.

White is the colour of one of the beast-gods, the tiger, whose cardinal direction is west. Often regarded as an ominous colour, white is associated with autumn, death, metal, weapons, war and punishment. The colour has always been a symbol of purity, immortality and mourning in China, with mourners at funerals wearing ceremonial clothing of undyed, unbleached natural white cloth.

Opposite During the Qing dynasty, vibrant colours were injected into the home. The understated ceramics and lacquerware of the Ming period were updated with the vivid colours.

Page 86 Yellow represents the earth and symbolizes nature, much as green does in the West. Yellow was reserved for the emperor and his retinue. Many ceramics, lacquered objects and textiles for the imperial household or the palace temples were coloured yellow.

Page 87 These gilded pebbles rest on a lacquered tray, their sheen reflected in its glossy surface. Gold filigree was often added to lacquer decorations, ebony and onyx to provide a luminous contrast.

Page 88 Contemporary Chinese designers often prefer muted colours or unfinished surfaces, as in this vernacular chair, exquisitely crafted in light-coloured wood. The base echoes the angular design of a Ming armchair. The cushion provides accents of crimson and black, visually softening the square base of the chair and adding texture to counterbalance the smooth surfaces around it.

Page 89 Linked with power and energy, red is associated with vitality and passion. It is also the colour of happiness.

Left Combined with subdued lighting, dark , sombre colours can create a relaxing mood, and transform a room into a quiet refuge.

Opposite A Western design, this bed combines the relaxing tones of white and beige associated with modernism and minimalism. In China, white has always been a symbol of purity, immortality and mourning. Classical Ming interiors and gardens featured whitewashed plaster and chalk-coloured stones.

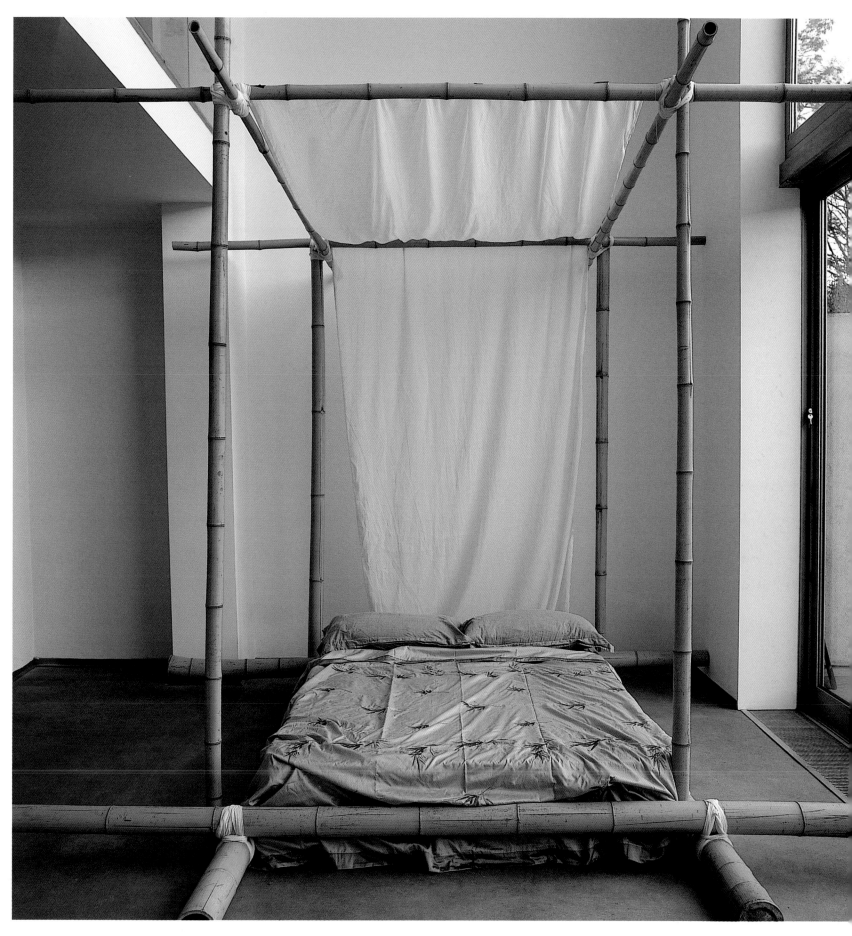

FURNITURE

傢具

FURNITURE

With the tales of luxury from the East came the lure of a particular type of treasure, which could bestow splendour on any Western interior: furniture. Impassioned collectors waited impatiently for the trading vessels to arrive with their holds full of cabinets, writing bureaux, mirror frames, dressing tables, console tables, stands and toilette cases. The distinctively shaped and decorated desks, screens, cupboards, chairs and beds featured richly lacquered surfaces, elegant curves and elaborate latticework – all exquisitely crafted from precious woods and often inlaid with jewels. The elegance of Ming furniture introduced a graceful simplicity to European homes, while the colourful lacquers and ornamentation of Qing style created an opulent look. Whereas Ming furniture is rarely decorated with auspicious symbols or motifs, the Manchus placed them on every imaginable surface, adorning Qing furniture with the lexicon of an invisible world. To early Western collectors, this mysterious symbolism and exotic imagery gave the works mystic connotations, and they often regarded Chinese furniture as enchanted objects.

Only recently has European furniture been as body conscious as the designs created during the Ming period. Chinese furniture was made according to the same considerations as a fashion garment, providing overall comfort to the body by supporting some areas and facilitating ease of movement in others. Chairs were designed to gently cradle the body, with the chair back curved just enough to support the spine, the chair arms extending to support the elbows and forearms, with the ends rounded into soft contours that embrace the palms of the hands. Most Ming furniture was proportioned to form an invisible box around the body, to centre and balance the posture from every direction. Holding oneself erect was believed to be a result of nature rather than of discipline; and correct posture was considered a sign of inner relaxation and health, where the qi of nature flowed through the body as it does through the landscape.

While Qing furniture is often described as heavy, elaborate and even garish, Ming pieces are characterized by their refinement and weightlessness. Furniture craftsmanship reached its peak during the Ming dynasty, when the fine quality of the wood and skilled workmanship created an elegance so distinctive that the Chinese refer to this era as the Classical period. Ming furniture continues to appear streamlined and contemporary today, largely because the treatment of the wood and the shape of the pieces seem familiar to modern sensibilities; Westerners are often surprised to learn that the style is over four hundred years old. The lines are so pure that experts in Chinese furniture can determine the age of a piece just by tapping and listening to the vibrations resonating through the wood.

The essence of Ming style was cultivated by scholars, artists and poets, who commissioned craftsmen to produce furniture reflecting their passion for the classical arts of literature, painting, calligraphy and gardening. Both the furniture and the architecture brought nature into an urban setting by emphasizing the processes of nature, its unity with the body and its rhythmic pulse. Wood was never considered to be static: movement was expressed in the subtle curve of each chair leg or armrest.

Throughout Chinese history, furniture has served a decorative and artistic function, indistinguishable from the house itself. The term for architecture is *damugong*, meaning 'large woodwork', while furniture is expressed as *xiaomugong*, or 'small woodwork'. Just as detail is an important aspect of a table or chair, each piece of furniture is considered an element essential to the interior. The walls, windows and doorways of the space, their architectural features and the function of the room are all closely related to the design and structure of the furniture used in the room. Like the house itself, period furniture was rarely constructed with nails, but was crafted instead by tongue-and-groove methods and mortise-and-tenon techniques. Rather than having to pack the furniture when the household moved, it could be taken apart and then reassembled in the new home. Houses, furniture and fine detailing were all crafted from the same woods, creating a harmonious continuity from micro to macro.

Chairs, in the form that we recognize them today, first appeared in China during the rise of the Tang dynasty. They evolved from an object akin to a collapsible camp stool, which had been brought to China in previous dynasties by invading tribes from the steppes of Asia. The Chinese crafted the seat out of woven rattan and adapted it to be carried over the shoulder, making it suitable for travelling or hunting. Over the years it evolved into ceremonial seats for high priests and thrones for emperors, replacing the dais and high platforms where they had traditionally sat.

With the eastward migration of Buddhism from India, chairs and raised platforms began to appear more frequently. The height of seats signified status: great masters would sit on elevated surfaces with their disciples gathered around them on low stools to study and recite scriptures. Hourglass-shaped stools made of straw and basketwork began to appear in the fourth century, and rattan stools made in a similar shape can still be found throughout modern China.

By the beginning of the Tang dynasty, stools and chairs had become common among the elite and those of rank and were starting to be used by the rest of the population. This signalled a turning point in Chinese interiors, which became distinct from those of Japan and the rest of Asia, sharing more similarities with Western homes.

Chairs are often made with seats much broader than those used in the West, to allow the Chinese to sit in the cross-legged 'lotus' position. Of these broad chairs, the *luohan* chair, which takes its name from an enlightened Buddhist monk, is characterized by its elegant horseshoe shape. Intended for an aged, wise person, it was traditionally crafted from a single piece of timber, with the wood steamed and bent into a dramatic curve that supported the back and sloped forwards into armrests. Today *luohan* chairs are generally made from willow wood, which carpenters cut into 7.5cm (3in) planks and steam to bend into the rounded form. Chairs from Shanxi province are characteristically decorated with carvings of landscapes, incense burners, floral motifs and mythic figures that reflect the influence of Buddhism.

The 'official's hat chair' – sometimes referred to as a 'scholar's chair' – is an armchair that takes its name from the similarity between the top horizontal rails protruding over the back posts of the chair, and the winged hats that were part of the formal dress worn by Ming officials.

Page 95 Fine Chinese furniture lends a special presence to a Western home, whether placed in an authentic setting or arranged with other styles. Originally designed to contain scrolls and official documents or store textiles and embroideries, this *maogui*, or cupboard, combines practical storage and understated elegance. Its even lines and muted lacquer finish present a rich contrast to the colourful wallpaper inspired by Chinese painting.

The 'yoke-back chair' is made without armrests, taking its name from the three-tiered rail fitted horizontally across the top of its back. Like the *luohan* chair, the width of the seat allows the legs to be crossed in the lotus position.

The rose chair is designed with a low back that can be placed in front of a latticed window, allowing those seated in it to be cooled by passing breezes or by leaning against the cool marble disc placed in its centre. The rounded carving of the back panel suggests the unfolding leaves of a rose as seen from above, hence the chair's name.

The placement of all furniture reflects the basic principles of architectural orientation, being traditionally arranged on a north–south axis with the most important chair facing south, in the direction of the front gate. This chair was generally large and imposing, and almost ceremonial in its role as the seat occupied by the head of the family. Furniture placement nearly always centred around the position of this important seat; other chairs and stools were aligned symmetrically on either side, with low tables placed between them.

Stools and footstools are made in a variety of shapes and sizes, and they often double as small tables or steps for reaching high shelves and cupboards. *Jiaju*, which literally means 'home tools', is a common word for this or any type of furniture used in a functional context. The cube-shaped stool from the Ming era is a brilliant combination of elegance, functionality and simplicity. Its efficient form gives it a contemporary profile in the West, while in China it has been regarded as a design classic for over five hundred years. The legs, base and top surface all merge together to form continuous lines, broken only by bending at right angles. The top surface is usually wood, but can also be crafted from cane, stone or a ceramic inlay, depending on the region where it is made. Most other types of stool are padded with thin seat cushions.

The height and shape of chairs and stools attest to the regions from which they originate. Low stools reflect the custom of sitting closer to the ground more common to temperate zones in the southern regions, while high chairs and footstools recall the northern climates where people sit well above the cold ground and the draughts blowing over the threshold. In the north of China, stools and footstools are often barrel-shaped and enclosed. Though made of wood, they are sometimes fitted with metal braziers inside, where lumps of burning coal warm those anchored to the seat.

A bed is more than a unique piece of furniture; it is a room within a room. At night it can be draped with fabric to become a private enclosure, and lined with fabric panels of wool or dense felt throughout the winter to block out cold draughts. In daytime the curtains are drawn back and the quilts folded away, and stools and low tables placed alongside for visiting guests.

Traditionally, when women gathered together it was most often in the private area of the home rather than in the formal rooms, where men often conducted business throughout the day and into evening. The bed was the centre of a woman's world, and the place from where she ruled her domain. The most important item in a bride's dowry, it was regarded as a status symbol among wives and concubines. On the wedding night, a small boy would be ritually rolled across the bed before the couple retired, in the hope that the bride would bear many male children during the marriage. The motifs decorating the bed also symbolized the desire for male progeny: depictions of clouds and rain represented sexual intercourse; the dragon, male virility. Because the lotus seedpod continues to grow even when the flower is in bloom, it also symbolized the early arrival of male children. The lotus bloom confirmed the bride's purity, with double lotus-shaped buds symbolizing her promise of chastity. Cross bars are never placed across the centre of the bed's roof in either direction, as an overhead beam is even believed to have the power to split a married couple apart by symbolically invoking the division of their union. The Chinese avoid hanging mirrors facing the bed, where they could drain away the *qi* of those reflected in their sleep.

Like the chair, the bed evolved from a low platform to a dais, and it still retains some of its ceremonial style. Beds are almost always enclosed on three sides of the base, symbolically blocking off space around those sleeping to protect them during the night. Simple railings and low panels of contoured wood are often fitted to the top of the base, rising in a slight arch or humpback shape across their centre. Pieces of intricate latticework stretch between the high posts to form a railing around the bed, and are sometimes fitted underneath the base as decorations or reinforcements. On Qing beds a lattice motif usually extends upwards alongside the posts, joining them together at the top by forming a plinth or a latticework roof.

The *luohan chang*, sometimes known as an opium bed, is undoubtedly the most comfortable piece of furniture in the formal rooms. As its name suggests, it is a long chair for reclining and sitting, similar to the Western *chaise longue*. As the largest and often the most splendid place to sit in the historic home, it made an ideal ceremonial chair for the head of the household. *Luohan chang* were seen as a kind of dais from which the elders could preside over the rest of the family. Qing versions were often elaborately carved and fitted with fretwork railings on three sides, though during the Ming period they were considerably less ornate.

Used primarily for sitting or reclining, some *luohan chang* can also be transformed into low tables by rolling away the cushions and textiles. The surfaces underneath are generally polished to a high gloss, covered in canework or rattan, or cut away altogether and fitted with an inset of woven ropes that form a springlike base. Apart from its pliable support, the woven inset is especially comfortable during the hot summer season. Woven surfaces were common throughout the Ming period and into the early Qing, although the best surviving examples of furniture from these periods are those with wooden panels. Woven seats gave way almost entirely to wooden ones during the eighteenth and nineteenth centuries, as the woven variety was less suited to the opulence of Qing style than to the simplicity of Ming.

The legs and feet of beds and *luohan chang* were generally much stronger than those of tables and chairs, as they had to support the extra weight and girth. If the legs were made of a hardwood they were often rounded and slightly contoured, ending in a horse's hoof or an orb held in the grip of a dragon's claw. If crafted in a softwood, the legs were generally made from slim planks of wood contoured into stylized 'cloud-head' feet, a shape that dates back to the Song dynasty. These mimicked the rolling cloud images featured in paintings and ceramics from this era, and were embellished with

This simple daybed is a streamlined version of the opium beds exported to the West in the last century. The daybed has been in use by the Chinese for many centuries. Couch beds were often designated as places of honour where the elders sat as they presided over family life, or were designed with four posts and a canopy roof that transformed them into a room within a room. They were usually constructed with a railing on three sides, or encircled by fretwork or carved wooden panels.

carved or lacquered swirls to suggest movement and depth. This dreamy motif was intended to make the bed appear to be floating in a mist, or soaring among the clouds like a flying carpet.

Traditionally, tables were shaped according to their function, and the literati rarely used them for more than one purpose. Painting, game playing, dining, writing or working is carried out on a table specifically designated for that activity, though in humble homes a single table may fulfil many functions. Round tables were typically made for dining, while long, narrow, rectangular tables were made as altars for the household shrine. The styles of these shrine tables vary from elaborate to simple, but most shrine tables flare sharply upwards on the two outermost edges, creating elegant curves on either side. The leg joins underneath are often concealed by carved brackets to give the top surface the appearance of a plinth. In Western homes, these are popularly used as hall tables today, where their slender width makes them particularly suited to narrow spaces.

Square tables fulfil a variety of functions, serving as desks for bureaucrats, scholars and artists, or as gaming tables for a group of four playing mah jong. When placed in the centre of the room and flanked by high-backed chairs, a square table is used as a gaming table. Pushed directly against a wall, placed under a window or positioned to face the door of the room, it is used as a table for writing or painting. A rectangular shape usually denoted a desk, which is deeper than a shrine but not as long; modern versions are fitted with Western-style shelves and drawers underneath. Side tables vary in size; the low and understated ones provide surfaces on which tea and trays of snacks can be served, while the tallest tables are used as plant stands or pedestals to hold incense burners.

Certain types of low table were constructed especially for use by those seated on the *kang* (a platform for sleeping on at night and reclining on by day), echoing the breakfast-trays used in the West. Though less common today, *kang* tables, desks and trays are made specifically to bridge the folded legs of those seated on the *kang*, and a range of special cabinets and stands are made to complement them. During the winter months in northern China, this type of furniture may completely replace the rest of the tables and chairs in the house, as the *kang*, warmed by the stove underneath, becomes the favourite spot for entertaining, relaxing, eating meals and sleeping. In summer *kang* furniture is taken outside for picnics, and used on boats where its lateral proportions are ideal for the confined space of the hold.

Because cupboards in a traditional Chinese home are seldom built into the architecture, the *maogui* is common to almost every household. Similar to the French armoire, *maogui* are sizeable free-standing cupboards in which folded clothes and textiles are stored. The Chinese name literally means 'hat cupboard', as originally these were where high-ranking officials stored their caps of office, medallions, beads and the many accessories they were required to wear. These are usually among the most treasured pieces found in a Chinese home today, often having been passed down from generation to generation, along with ancestor portraits and dowry beds.

Food cupboards were often built with vents and openings that allowed air to circulate. The term for these translates as 'enraging the cat', because the tiny openings in the surface allowed a cat to see and smell the food within, but not to reach inside.

Folding lacquer screens are the crowning glory of Chinese furniture; the craftsmanship and precious materials are unparalleled. Here, a six-panelled screen (top left) contains inlays of mother-of-pearl in its depiction of a romantic moonlit garden, while on another screen (bottom right) images from the natural world are etched across the lacquer surface in gold leaf. The trim bordering the surface of the *kang* table (top right) is raised to hold objects in place as it is carried from the *kang* to serve food in other parts of the house. The trim on the desk (bottom left) is flush with the surface to allow the scholar to move easily across it while writing or painting.

Wood

The frenzy of construction and furniture-making that resulted from the aesthetically inclined Ming craft movement almost depleted native supplies of luxury hardwoods. After an imperial ban on maritime trade was finally lifted in 1567, most furniture was produced from the tropical hardwoods imported from Burma, Thailand and India into the ports of Shanghai and Canton. It was the use of these heavy, dense woods that accelerated advances in joinery techniques throughout the late Ming and early Qing periods, creating weightless, elegant forms that had been previously unattainable in softwood.

The bulk of the Chinese furniture in today's market is crafted from softwoods typically sourced by local craftsmen. This is why many softwood pieces either are made in a 'vernacular' style – a design typical of a specific region or area – or are based on classical pieces that have been adapted to local sensibilities. Although timber-growing regions are spread far apart, the network of rivers in central and southern China and the rail network in the north make it possible to circulate most precious woods to workshops throughout the country. The provinces of Hubei, Jiangxi and Sichuan are most famous for their hardwoods, but the growing problem of deforestation in these areas means that timber from other parts of South-east Asia continues to be imported in order to meet the demand.

Because hardwood was usually chosen for its durability, its translucency of colour and the satin lustre of its finish, it is associated more with luxury than vernacular style. In this case, hardwood furniture was not necessarily produced in the region where hardwoods grew, as they were harvested for consignment to regions where there were craftsmen skilled enough to work them. This is why the honey-coloured *huanghuali*, or yellow rosewood, furniture was thought to originate from Jiangsu province – despite the fact that the wood itself was probably harvested on the island of Hainan – as specialist craftsmen during the Ming and Qing periods assembled in Jiangsu province to make tables, chairs, panels and screens from it.

The furniture-making of China was superior to that of European craftsmen. While the furniture of great Western cabinetmakers like Chippendale was often merely painted, varnished and adorned with finials, Chinese craftsmen took delight in finishing their work with carvings, patterned inlays, lacquering and metalwork trim. The door jambs of cupboards and cabinets were subtly contoured, and fitted with doors containing panel inlays or exquisite reliefs.

Beds were fenced with fretted palings and intricate latticework, and tables and chairs were buttressed by arched brackets and delicate joints. The frames of tables, chairs and beds were mitred together by joints concealed among subtle moulding carved into the wood.

Woods were celebrated for the natural beauty of their grains and their aromatic properties throughout the whole of the Ming period. The woods chosen for fine furniture were characterized by their natural finishes, which were left untreated but polished to a high sheen. Non-aromatic wood was often coated in clear lacquer to protect it from woodworm, termites, moisture and discoloration. The coloured lacquers applied in the Qing period obscured the grain of the wood altogether, transforming furniture into rich

The detail hidden in this example of Ming fretwork attests to the subtle beauty that characterized carved wood throughout the Ming period. Carefree musicians dance and sing in a forest glade, incorporating representations of harmony and joy into the pattern. The fretwork around them transmutes into gargoyle-like creatures, symbolically poised at the four corners of the earth, they ward off evil from every direction.

Left Nests of tables have been crafted in wood continuously for several millennia. The early nomadic peoples inhabiting the north of China created simple, modular furniture from lightweight softwoods that could be easily stored and quickly assembled. These contemporary nests, shown against a display alcove created by wooden cladding, give a timely update to classical Chinese pieces.

Opposite As well as being crafted into fine pieces of furniture, beautiful woods were used to produce functional items. Robust and hard-wearing, *zhazhen* was often used for chests of drawers (top left) and could be left untreated. This ladder (far right) imitates a functional design, but the black bamboo it is made from transforms its rustic shape into an elegant feature. It was more common to lacquer large tables and chests in black than to make them from wood, and they often had intricate motifs inlaid into their surfaces (bottom left) rather than carvings.

works of baroque splendour. The lacquered surfaces lent themselves to further embellishment, and the furniture from this period was frequently finished with swirling patterns, filigree etchings and auspicious symbols applied in gold leaf.

The Chinese often credit their craft expertise to the guidance of Lu Ban, the patron deity of cabinetmakers and craftsmen, based on the historical figure of Gong Ban, who was a master carpenter in the kingdom of Lu during the fourth century BC. The mythic tales of his adventures portray him as a genius mechanic and craftsman, inventor of the carpenter's sawhorse, the saw, and a variety of other tools and utensils still used today. In art and literature Lu Ban is portrayed as a wandering artisan, mysteriously appearing to bless craftsmen with his advice on how to overcome problems. Legend has it that his blessings extend to those who purchase the final product – they can even call upon Lu Ban to solve the problems of interior decoration after the furniture is taken home!

Precious to Chinese furniture makers are those woods with hues of deep purple, dark red and dense black. Of these, the rare *zitan*, or purple sandalwood, native to southern China has always been especially treasured. The wood is extremely dense, with a deep, fine grain that becomes dark purple in tone when polished to a high sheen. *Zitan* would be sanded and coated in a fine powder to fill any open pores. As it doesn't have the fragrance associated with true sandalwood, it is usually coated with a clear layer of uncoloured lacquer to emphasize its silky shimmer.

Zitan closely resembles *huali*, or rosewood, which rivals it in beauty and lustre. Traditionally, *huali* and *zitan* were cut from the lush tropical forests on the island of Hainan, but today these woods are imported from tropical forests in other parts of South-east Asia. The rich reddish colour and beautiful black markings of the *hongdoumu*, or 'red bean tree', from the Sichuan region are often likened to those of *huali* and *zitan*, but its density makes it more akin to teak. The *hongdoumu* is so dense that it will actually sink in water, meaning it has to be transported overland rather than floated downstream. The variegated *jichimu* wood is unique in having two different textures when cut.

Cypress has been highly prized since the Song dynasty for its lustrous sheen and aromatic fragrance. Its surface has a distinctive waxy or oily feel, its grain is generally quite straight and evenly textured, and the wood is highly resistant to rot and insect infestation. Connoisseurs of fine furniture in the Ming period cited cypress as a favourite. During the Qing dynasty the southern cypress was considered on a par with *nanmu*, which means 'southern wood' and is Chinese cedar; *nanmu* was widely used in the construction of the Yuanmingyuan palaces in Beijing. The heartwood of weeping cypress has a golden-brown tonality, sometimes with reddish streaks. As the cut wood matures, the colour of the heartwood deepens, while the sapwood retains its paler tonalities.

Camphor wood, or *zhangmu*, has a long history of use for wardrobes and storage chests. The strong scent of camphor wood, which repels insects, diminishes very little over time. The interlocking woodgrain produces a contrasting pattern of dark lines against a light background. The hefty wood from its thickest roots was often used to construct cabinets, their dense surfaces polished to a rich lustre. The pale sapwood of camphor is clearly distinguished from the heartwood, whose burgundy-brown colour is typically figured with reddish lines and darker hues.

Wood was highly valued for its grain and colouring, and its beauty was often combined with other materials. This rose chair (top right) has a disc of smooth stone set into the back, while the subtle auburn tones of the latticework screen behind it are offset by the panel of green lacquer it encases. The back, sides and seat of this extraordinary armchair (bottom right) are upholstered with leather, emphasizing the dark grain in the wood of its fan-like 'wings'. This tall cupboard (left), with its intricate lattice insets, displays the dark lustre characteristic of *hongmu*, the wood commonly known as Chinese mahogany.

Lacquer

Lacquerware was developed in China in ancient times, but rose to its peak during the Yuan dynasty, as craftsmen learned to layer the material to unprecedented thickness and give their decorations a sculptural feel. The lacquered objects made during the Ming dynasty often featured intricate designs and subtle motifs, but by the Qing period they depicted complex pictorial scenes and popular auspicious iconography. Europe has imported lacquerwork from Asia from about 1600.

Chinese lacquer, which is a highly polished, opaque varnish applied to wood, comes from the sap extracted from the lacquer tree, *Rhus vernicifera*. This is native to southern and central China and is a close relative of North American poison ivy. Until it has set and dried, the raw lacquer in liquid form is toxic to the skin, creating a reaction similar to that caused by touching poison ivy. The Chinese worked lacquer with special tools to avoid contact. The liquid sap would dry out on the long journey west, making it impossible to export to Europe. Lacquer equivalents were found in parts of southern Europe, but these lacked the lustrous sheen that characterized Chinese lacquerware.

Lacquer has to be applied in thin coats, each of which is allowed to harden and is rubbed smooth before the next is applied. Craftsmen begin with a low-grade lacquer and save the best qualities for the final coats. Lacquer can be coloured by adding pigments, red and black being the most widely used in China.

Its unique properties make lacquer ideal as a protective and decorative coating, and as a malleable surface which can be incised and filled with metal, stone and shell. As early as the twelfth century, lacquered furniture was adorned with pieces of mother-of-pearl cut into shapes and figures, often used with gold foil to construct designs prized for their delicacy and precision.

But lacquer is far more than just a glossy coating for wood; it is also a material that can be shaped, sculpted and carved. Though Japan learned the art of lacquerwork from China, the technique of carving it was unique to Chinese craftsmen. Thick sheets are created for this purpose by applying multiple layers. Because of the time and skill required to prepare raw lacquer, and the labour-intensive processes of layering, burnishing and carving, lacquerware was originally a luxury item found only in wealthy homes.

During the Ming and Qing dynasties, the palace workshops controlled the work of the resident artisan families as well as a large number of craftsmen working in the provinces. The palace lacquers produced during this time were often inscribed with reign titles and cyclical dates, and the imperial symbols continued to be an important characteristic of lacquerware throughout the Ming and Qing dynasties – possibly the earliest form of label chic. As the decorative industries in the coastal ports grew, many craftsmen trained in the palace workshops left to work commercially on export goods. The style of work they did and the decorative motifs they used changed to suit the demands of the West, and some of these hybrid designs were even purchased for the imperial palaces as tokens of 'Europeanoiserie'.

Lacquer screens known as Coromandels were made in China and shipped to Europe via India's Coromandel coast from the seventeenth century. Consisting of up to twelve carved wooden panels coated with a lacquer finish, the screens are delicately engraved, painted and ornamented. They are still produced in China today.

Although the glossy surfaces of this rustic wooden table and leather hatbox resemble black lacquerware, their appearance results from the coats of clear lacquer applied to protect them against infestation and decay. Clear lacquer was often applied to natural wood as a preservative, allowing the beauty of its grain to remain visible beneath its glossy surface.

Bamboo

Throughout Chinese history, scholars and philosophers alike have extolled the virtues of the bamboo, describing it as 'the most humble of woods' and 'the most virtuous of plants'. Just as the poet Tao Qian inspired the literati to romanticize the simple, rustic lifestyle of the peasantry, so too did they learn to revere the aesthetic simplicity of bamboo. Renowned painters chose bamboo as a subject – as they still do today – often depicting it alongside a pool of water, or in the moist terrain in which this woody grass grows. One of the earliest literary references to bamboo was recorded in the *Shijing*, or 'Book of Songs', poetically recounting the beauty of a vibrantly green bamboo tree viewed from across water.

Bamboo has a multitude of purposes: it is flexible enough to be used as fishing rods, strong enough to create ladders and scaffolding, and beautiful enough to craft in fine furniture or to hang exquisite textiles from. The trunk and limbs grow in straight lengths, making it particularly valuable for furniture. Its hollow centre gives it musicality too – bamboo pieces can be played as percussion instruments or made into flutes. Chefs delight in its antibacterial properties, which make it ideal for use as cooking utensils and chopsticks, and its young shoots are even edible.

It has been in use for at least ten thousand years – bamboo objects have been unearthed that date back to the Neolithic period. Even then bamboo was used for both practical purposes and ornamentation: hairpins, arrow sheaths, tools and utensils are among early implements made from it.

Bamboo belongs to a family of evergreen plants of which there are over a thousand varieties. The colour of its wood ranges from light tan to dark brown, reddish-tinted or sometimes deep auburn. Often the wood is darkest around its nodes, with light patches in between them, creating a variegated effect. The bamboo grown in Sichuan is known for its delicate pattern, while the variety found in Hangzhou has been described as deep purple in colour. The bamboo native to Guangdong and Guangxi has palm-like leaves that can be crafted into screens and shutters when dried.

Bamboo furniture is popular in all types of homes, and is used both indoors and outdoors. In southern China, bamboo chairs abound, the most common being the low-seat, high-back type. Their simplicity introduces a rustic element to the homes of the wealthy, where they are placed alongside sophisticated pieces, and over time develop the same luminous patina. The affordability of bamboo makes it the staple furniture of humble homes, especially in rural areas.

Each piece is constructed from lengths of varying thickness, with the broadest pieces used to form the frame, and thinner ones forming slats for the seat and back, or narrow pins that secure the entire frame. Traditionally, the lengths of bamboo are bound together with fibres rather than being nailed.

Like the willow that is steamed and bent to fashion the *luohan* chair (see page 96), bamboo also becomes pliable when heated, to the extent that a single length can be bent into right angles to form a square base or half of the frame. Usually a segment has to be partially cut away to allow the wood to bend into a right angle, creating a recess that doubles as an interlocking join. These steaming techniques mean that fewer cuts and joins are necessary in bamboo furniture.

The versatility of bamboo enables it to assume a multitude of shapes and forms. Here, a vernacular armchair with an integral footstool has been created by bending and steaming the pliable bamboo into shape. The crescent-shaped wall is panelled with the timber harvested from a grove of young bamboo, while the flooring beneath is constructed from narrow planks of mature bamboo to provide a durable and attractive surface.

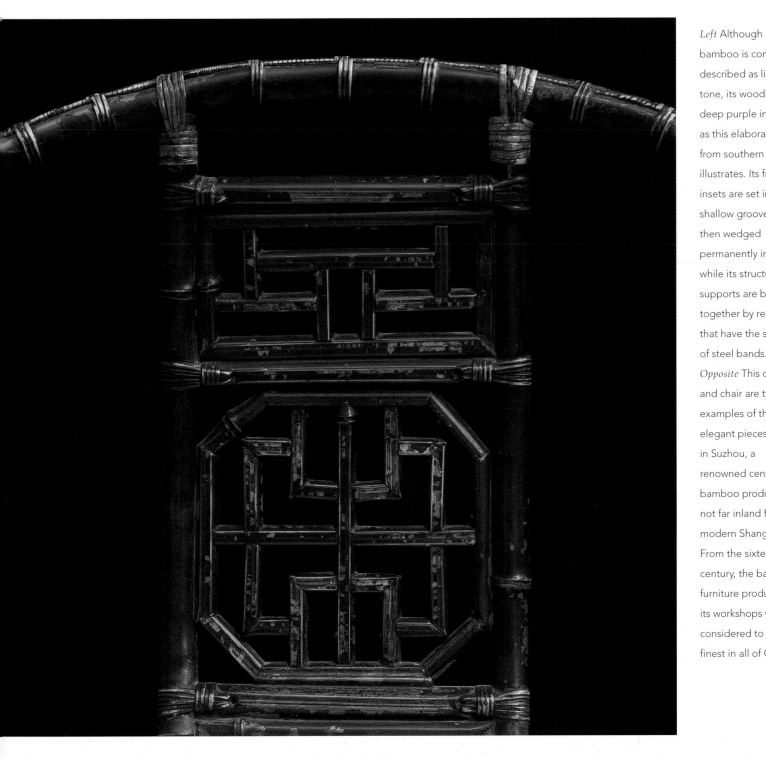

Left Although bamboo is commonly described as light in tone, its wood can be deep purple in colour, as this elaborate chair from southern China illustrates. Its fretwork insets are set into shallow grooves and then wedged permanently in place, while its structural supports are bound together by reeds that have the strength of steel bands.

Opposite This desk and chair are typical examples of the elegant pieces made in Suzhou, a renowned centre for bamboo production not far inland from modern Shanghai. From the sixteenth century, the bamboo furniture produced in its workshops was considered to be the finest in all of China.

Detail

Details play a central role in Chinese furniture. Whether used for practicalities like hinges, handles and corner mounts, or the springy comfort of canework, they were planned into the overall aesthetic at the design stage. The combination of materials became more sophisticated after the ban on imported wood was lifted in the sixteenth century, making great quantities of tropical hardwood available to Chinese craftsmen, who had primarily been working with native softwoods. No longer was it necessary to apply multiple coats of lacquer over the wood for protection and decoration, as had been the case when softwoods were prevalent. The hardness of the wood gave cabinetmakers the perfect material for carving elaborate designs and reliefs. Hardwoods leant themselves to such detailing as inlays of precious stones, tortoiseshell and rare wood, and were strong enough to support mounts made of bronze, brass and other metals used to decorate corners and disguise joints.

Stone was a popular material for decorative panels fitted into chairs, table tops and screens. Marble, serpentine and granite were commonly used; agate, jade, malachite, nephrite and lapis lazuli were more rare. The patterns of nature revealed in these slices of geological time were often regarded as an abstract landscape scene or a vision of the mineral kingdom.

Ceramic panels were sometimes used in table tops in place of stone. These could be left unglazed to mimic coarse stone, or they could be decorated to depict landscapes, figures or motifs.

Metal hardware was commonly used for reinforcement and decoration. Even in ancient times, ironmongery was a specialized guild that had more in common with science than with woodworking. Chinese metalsmiths were skilled in firing decorative hardware to perfection, but were also preoccupied with complex metallurgical formulas to create alloys that had unsurpassed strength and a range of different hues.

The hardware handles made for lattice doors, cupboard doors and drawers depicted a variety of animals, fish and birds. Fish symbolized harmony and freedom during the Ming dynasty. They were heavily romanticized by the philosophers and scholars of the era, who imagined them to be completely content in their underwater kingdom, free of restraint as they followed the course of nature. Fish also featured in the etchings and engravings adorning locks and keys, which were commonly regarded as signs of status and wealth. The keys used by high-ranking officials and members of rich households were beautifully and artistically made, depicting images of *qilins* (the auspicious Chinese unicorn), butterflies, tigers and panthers.

Locksmith craftsmanship reached its peak during the Tang dynasty, when locks were valuable pieces of equipment, and materials like bronze, silver or gold were often used. Tang locks were mostly padlocks that opened by keys or by combinations. Often the keyhole was hidden among tiny crevices decorating the lock's surface so that only the owner could find it immediately. Chinese combination locks were different from those made in the West, as the rotating wheels usually bore symbols rather than numbers, or poetic words that had to form a nonsensical phrase to open. Keys were also a symbol of married women; because married women were designated as the family's 'key-carriers', women who did not have a key fastened to their robes were assumed to be unmarried.

Locks and metal hardware were regarded as signs of status and wealth. Produced in brass alloy, bronze, nickel, silver and gold, they were used to ornament handles and hinges and also to act as decorations. The three plates and set of hinges shown here are cast in *paktong*, a brass alloy containing a small amount of nickel to retard the tarnishing characteristic of pure brass. Set against luminous black and ruby red, *paktong* almost takes on the lustre of gold. The fastenings shown in the top and bottom left-hand pictures can be secured by fitting a lock through the loop. The pull tabs shown in the bottom left-hand picture represent fish, which symbolized harmony and freedom during the Ming era.

TEXTILES

紡織

TEXTILES

The textiles of China have always been considered some of the most resplendent and colourful ever produced, as renowned in the ancient world as they were at the height of chinoiserie. Even before the Chinese began trading ceramics, spices and lacquerware, the sumptuous fabrics acquired by Mediterranean and Middle Eastern traders created a mythology more outlandish than the tall tales of the East India merchants. The Romans traded with a land they called Serica, the land of silk, so remote and mysterious that mere mortals feared to journey beyond its borders, fearing the lithe tigers and fearsome dragons that roamed its motifs.

These legends and mysteries were perpetuated well into the Han dynasty, largely because the Chinese were the only people who possessed the secrets of silk weaving. By that time they had established lucrative export markets to trade directly with Asia and the Middle East. The legendary caravan route that carried goods overland is known today as the Silk Route, following a term coined in the late nineteenth century to describe the trading paths that ran west from China through Central Asia to Turkey and Syria, then by sea to ports in Europe. Silk was but one of the many expensive, sought-after luxuries carried along the Silk Route: elaborate tapestries and intricate embroideries stitched with stories of frivolity and fantasy were sold alongside carpets, brocades and needlework ablaze with crimson and gold.

By the end of the third century, bandit raids threatened these routes; until the seventh century, overland routes to China were too dangerous to attempt without garrison escorts. As Western sea merchants rarely sailed beyond the Black Sea, trade between East and West was sporadic. Not until the thirteenth-century conqueror Genghis Khan re-established links between China and the West did the great mercantile companies of Venice, Pisa and Genoa return to trade with China, mostly in silk.

Bales of silk were regularly exported from China throughout the Yuan dynasty, transported to Europe across Asia and the Middle East. Cloths of gold, silks, delicate embroidery and intricate quilting whetted European appetites for the looms of Cathay. Fabrics adorned with lions, phoenixes and dragons were often used by the Catholic clergy at that time, and these motifs were imitated by weavers in Europe on tapestries and furnishings. Suddenly China closed its doors on foreigners again; the xenophobic policies of the Ming dynasty were virtually to seal China off for another few centuries.

During this long embargo, the demand for silk, embroideries, tapestries and printed cottons continued. European weavers attempted to imitate the splendours of Chinese textiles by producing their own ranges of cloth, which mimicked everything from Buddhist robes to Indian chintzes and Persian carpets. Chintz, the printed cotton exported to Europe from India in the sixteenth and seventeenth centuries, was mistakenly attributed to the chintzes produced in Canton. When imitations were produced in France and England, these were given the generic title of *façon de la Chine*. Indian chintzes popularized the 'Tree of Life' design, and this was later copied in the workshops of Canton at the request of European merchants. They falsely assigned it to the pantheon of chinoiserie motifs as an icon of China.

By the second half of the seventeenth century the East India Company had arrived in England bearing richly embroidered silk hangings stitched with yarns of gleaming gold and silver set amid brilliant jewel colours and soft, gossamer threads. The charter of the East India Company established links with the textile merchants of China through the port of Canton. Ships would anchor at Madras or Bombay on the long journey east, taking Indian fabrics, Buddhist relics and polished jewels on board which they later exchanged for the bolts of silk and embroideries that were to be exported to Europe or back to India.

With the Baroque in full swing in Europe, the brilliance of Chinese fabrics contributed greatly to the extravagance, luxury and romance lavished on the interiors of the period. Chinese embroideries were hung from floor to ceiling in drawing rooms, libraries and ballrooms, draped over bed frames and capped with billowing plumes of feathers. These embroideries and tapestries were often the subject of conversation during the newly fashionable pastime of drinking tea – a ritual which, to be complete, required china teapots and lacquered trays.

As the fashion for hanging textiles grew, Chinese fabrics were draped at windows and doors, canopied over settees and hung on the walls. Lengths of painted taffeta were fixed to the wall by stretching them over wooden frameworks, which were then mounted side-by-side as panels, or positioned around the room as though they were overlarge paintings. The most elaborate of these were framed in outlines of faux bamboo or carved trim that mimicked Ming fretwork. The panels of fabric may have decorated the room in a single motif, or each one may have depicted a different design.

Genre scenes of the Chinese emperor and his coterie were popular, as were the brooding mandarins that strolled amid exotic landscapes with umbrella-carrying ladies and their diminutive attendants. These chinoiserie figures seemed preoccupied with drinking tiny pots of tea, smoking pipes of tobacco, catching butterflies and climbing pagodas. The fishing party was to become a favourite theme for chinoiserie fabrics, while arched bridges, bamboo poles and pools of cascading water remained popular throughout the eighteenth century and beyond.

The magic and mystery of Cathay slowly disappeared as the early eighteenth-century looms of London's Spitalfields and Lyon in France produced silk closer to home. Figured silks were among those first woven in Europe, mostly featuring motifs etched in gold or silver thread against a damask background, with foliage and floral designs. The style was set by the active imagination and exquisite draughtsmanship of Jean Pillement, a French *maître d'art* who created hundreds of chinoiserie motifs for hanging textiles and soft furnishings. In the 1750s he set the style for Rococo chinoiserie in London and in Paris, decorating many Rococo rooms with printed linen, or his freehand drawings on cotton and silk. Some of Pillement's most stunning works have been preserved in the staterooms of the sprawling palaces of Oranienbaum, the summer estate of the Russian tsars built on the Gulf of Finland. The fabrics lining the walls of the Glass Bead Room were embroidered with Pillement designs drawn across thick silks. Pillement's willowy trees and giant flowers wind delicately through other-worldly landscapes lavishly covered with two million glass beads coloured in hues of sapphire, ruby and amethyst.

Page 119 The tapestries, brocades and needlework that merchants traded on the Silk Route filled palaces all over the ancient world. The Chinese continue to embrace their rich textile heritage today, with silken wall hangings, cushion covers, embroidered textiles and furniture upholstery. In this Chinese home, a collection of silk cushions featuring embroidered flowers is framed by heavy damask curtains emblazoned with auspicious symbols and lined with Siamoise fabric. A traditional wedding-bed coverlet is stretched across the divan.

Like the ornaments that moved further and further away from the original Chinese designs, chinoiserie textiles also expressed a purely European vision of the mythical Cathay invented by the West. The striped fabric known as Siamoise, a design modelled on the 'Chinese' robes worn by the Siamese ambassadors to the court of Louis XIV, was a favourite of the French and Germans, but far removed from genuine Chinese styles. Pékin, also French, was a brocade with a pattern of Northern European flora woven amidst the alternating matt and shiny bands of the silk. The French textiles known as toiles de Jouy were used to cover chairs, beds and walls, and printed in monochrome using an engraved copper plate. This was the reverse of the Chinese woodblock printing method, as the dye was transferred onto the fabrics from the incised areas of the plate rather than from a relief image, as on the woodblock. Featuring pictorial scenes, many of them chinoiserie fantasies, toiles de Jouy were often embellished with festoons of flowers and trailing ribbons that would have been unknown to the Chinese.

European textile artists typically decorated chinoiserie fabrics with elaborate fretwork patterns as background elements, their geometry creating a subtle repeating pattern that circled family crests or classical emblems. Trailing flowers, exotic plants, swirling water, trees with sweeping branches and shrubs with tropical-looking flora and foliage brought nature to life. Vases and ornaments set on carved stands, figures dressed in ceremonial robes and colourful birds were often used as stand-alone motifs, as were, curiously, pineapples. These patterns almost always included architecture of some sort: palaces, shrines, teahouses and pagodas featured in landscapes interspersed with cloud-capped mountains, gnarled trees and zigzag bridges.

It is hard to imagine the reaction of the Chinese if these Western methods and motifs had been brought back to decorate a Chinese home. Textiles in the Chinese interior were used in a different way altogether – although they were often richly embellished, they acted as an accent rather than a decorative feature. It was a common practice in China to drape fabric over wooden furniture in the winter months, and the back rail capping Ming chairs was designed to support an ample width of fabric that would hang over the back and seat before continuing to the floor. In keeping with the motifs characteristic of Ming style, the designs of these fabrics emphasized form and line rather than ornamentation; they were often decorated with little more than a band of contrasting colour around the edges. The textiles used to insulate the walls, windows and doors were hung flush against them, rather than being gathered and draped as was fashionable in Europe. Even the fabrics adorning bed frames were hung with spartan simplicity, providing privacy and insulation rather than decorative swags.

Although the soft furnishings decorating the Chinese home during the Qing period were more elaborate than Ming fabrics, they adorned the interior with the same fluidity, moving from bed frame to chair to window as the weather dictated. On milder days they could be easily packed away. As there were no built-in cupboards, cabinets and chests in many shapes and sizes were used to store fabrics. The wardrobes and hat cupboards described on page 100 were comprised of upper and lower units, the doors of each fitted with a removable central stile so that bolts of fabrics, folded garments and rolls of bedding could be stored across the entire width of the shelves without wrinkling.

The streamlined elegance of Ming style resurfaced in the late nineteenth/early twentieth century through the textiles of Art Nouveau. Art Nouveau was mostly derived from Gothic and Rococo, which itself had roots in chinoiserie, and from the arts of the East. Much of the enigmatic form, elegance and colour for which Art Nouveau is famous can be related to the spirit of Ming design. Art Nouveau was characterized by stylized patterns and motifs taken primarily from nature, representing a controlled exuberance of form, line and colour that mimicked the balance of Chinese designs. The cresting

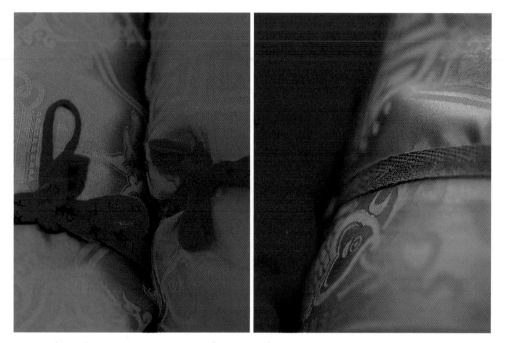

Below left Colourful Chinese cottons and silks are widely used for home furnishings in the West – many designers travel to fabric fairs in China and ship them home by the roll.

Opposite The image of Chairman Mao, the first chairman of the People's Republic of China, was given pop-art status by Andy Warhol. It was then transformed into a fashion icon by Vivienne Tam, the New York-based fashion designer originally from Hong Kong. More recently, Chairman Mao's portrait has achieved kitsch value, featuring on curtains, cushion covers, book jackets and lampshades.

waves, lotus leaves and curvaceous floral motifs were arranged in abstract patterns and repeated on fabrics and wall hangings, or symmetrically arrayed along the edging of upholstery furnishings.

The passion for antique and vintage textiles persists to the present day, and many contemporary interiors feature Chinese textiles as draperies and upholstery, or display antique robes as wall hangings. Today, Chinese furniture, ceramics and works of art are all avidly collected, but textiles are less known and less appreciated. Many 'modern' patterns popular in China today are derived from motifs dating back to the Song and Tang dynasties, but eighteenth-century Qing motifs are by far the most common. North American fabric designers are also beginning to find inspiration in the motifs of China's rich history, depicting them in bright colours against a strong background.

Western textile designers have a long history of finding inspiration in the chinoiserie vogue that thrived on illusion and misrepresentation. This is changing as contemporary textile designers embark on a quest for authenticity unknown to the chinoiserie weavers of previous centuries. Though some designers are recreating the chinoiserie motifs of seventeenth- and eighteenth-century interiors, many others tend to be true to authentic designs, researching and preserving the Chinese motifs of previous eras. While some of these are artfully reworked into new designs, others are painstakingly preserved to reflect the rich tradition that gives them a style of their own.

Above The mystique associated with Chinese fabrics slowly dissipated as European looms produced silk closer to home. Foliage and floral designs, as in the fabric used to upholster these chairs, were among the first types woven in Europe. The early Western chinoiserie textiles were also stretched over a framework of battens and fixed to the walls. This interior replicates the style in the modern day.

Opposite The European passion for Chinese textiles has persisted through the centuries and continues to the present day. Some enthusiasts claim to sleep in nothing but Chinese silk, collecting antique and vintage bedding like the embroidered textiles shown here. This cushion, set amid silk fabrics (top left), captures two serpentine dragons. The quilted coverlet (top right) is a single piece of hand-stitched cotton, layered over a cotton sheet embroidered with crimson chrysanthemums. Woven silk fabrics (bottom left) have been cut for their next life as cushion covers, while cushions (bottom right) feature foliage embroidery inspired by an autumn sunset.

Carpets

Chinese carpets have their own distinctive style, characterized by their dense texture, their silky surface and the contours cut into their rug pile to create elegant reliefs. Their long lifespan means that even delicate silk carpets survive their owners by several centuries, improving with age and becoming collectible items. Many nineteenth-century carpets from the Qing dynasty remain in excellent condition today, attributed in part to the practice of removing them from the floor when they were not in use. Carpets were almost never permanent fixtures – they were moved from room to room and from bed to chair, and were often taken with the owners when they travelled.

The bold patterns of Chinese carpets inject energy into the core of any room, whether it is a contemporary setting or a period-style interior. Their patterns range from simple geometric designs and abstract shapes to bold, stylized medallions and familiar floral patterns. Many of the abstract and geometric patterns used by the Chinese were created by the ancient weavers of Central Asia, revealing the influence of primeval symbols from Khotan and the Caucasus. Chequerboard designs, crosses, diagonals and lozenges are combined with figurative images and patterns from nature. Medallion patterns are also derived from the ancient motifs of Central Asia and from similar emblems featured on silk brocades and Chinese porcelain. Traditional floral designs which mimic the motifs of Chinese silk textiles have always been popular. Lotus flowers are popular features, freely combined with dragons, phoenixes, clouds, waves and mountains.

Large carpets, particularly woollen ones, were not used in China until relatively recent times. The early carpets were usually small so that they could be carried easily by the steppe nomads as they were used during the different daily activities. A single carpet provided a sleeping place, a tablecloth, a seat, a base for spiritual or devotional practice and a saddle for riding horseback.

In northern China during the Tang period, small rugs were woven to cover the *kang* (see page 100) and to provide comfortable seating, but sometimes these were extended to cover the whole surface of the *kang*. Most of these carpets were made of felt, yak hair or fine camel down, and typically dyed black and red at the borders. These *kang* carpets are thought to be the earliest surviving examples of authentic Chinese carpets.

By the Ming dynasty, temple floor mats, prayer rugs and decorative carpets were also made in northern China, woven mostly from wool and camel down. Some early Ming carpets still survive today, made in wool pile and woven with Buddhist designs, whose colours still remain bright despite the passage of time. At the height of the trade along the Silk Route, the Chinese provinces bordering it provided carpets to sell to foreign merchants, competing against goods woven in Tibet and Mongolia, both of which were famous for the beauty of their carpets.

China's exportation of carpets slowed down through the centuries as the demand for silk and ceramics increased. In the early 1900s the industry was revitalized, and China continues to export both old and new carpets today. Antique Chinese carpets can be bought in the West at auction or from specialist dealers, who provide certification of provenance and authenticity if the item is valuable. Like a work of art, a carpet is an investment and a treasure – but one that can actually be used as its value increases.

This antique folding chair, also called a hunting chair because of the collapsible design that made it easily transported by a mounted huntsman, rests amidst a multitude of butterflies seemingly hovering above a carpet of interlocking geometric shapes. Butterflies are traditionally depicted in a floral, rather than geometric, environment. The money plant on the chair is considered to be auspicious.

Above In this silken carpet, a flock of chirping swallows lands in a field of poppies. Chinese carpets are often too beautiful to decorate the floor, but on the wall they provide an exotic backdrop that fuels the imagination.

Page 130 A hanging carpet made at the height of Chairman Mao's reign is imbued with patriotic zeal for China's great leap forward. Ceremonial red lanterns hang from the eaves to denote an official holiday, while a red Communist flag flies outside a public building. During the Communist era, China did not halt the production of luxury goods, but replaced many 'decadent' motifs with political imagery.

Page 131 These hanging carpets portray two very different visions of China. The top carpet depicts a public assembly to celebrate Maoist ideology, complete with modern vehicles and Western clothing. The bottom carpet captures the tranquil water garden once enjoyed by a wealthy landowner, representing the beauty of China's artistic heritage.

Opposite While carpets from the Qing dynasty included a broad range of motifs, the dragon was the most popular icon of the era. The fearsome dragon articulated in this design winds its way through an ethereal world laden with auspicious symbolism that appeals to the literati's taste for classical imagery. A grain vessel is filled with a measure of millet in the top left-hand corner, and a pestle and mortar is depicted immediately below it; these are associated with riches and scholarly interests respectively. Butterflies and other insects circle the dragon, while the scrolling clouds below denote its other-worldly status. The wavy motifs at the bottom of the textile are cosmic rays: emanating upwards, they endow the dragon with protective qualities and spiritual harmony.

Hanging Fabrics

Early wall hangings were used to depict religious and ethical teachings in ancient China, and were embroidered with the same auspicious symbols as the ritual objects associated with Taoism, Confucianism and Buddhism. This changed during the Song dynasty, when some tapestries were made for purely decorative purposes. Their designs became richer and more stylized as they were embellished with brushwork and embroidery, making the Song period the golden age of tapestries in China. The tapestries of the Yuan dynasty featured threads of silver and gold for an opulent effect, while Ming tapestries revived the simple, classical designs of Song textiles. By the end of the Ming period, weavers had refined their techniques considerably to create works with detailed compositions and neatly textured surfaces.

Tapestries of the Qing dynasty featured a broader range of motifs than previous eras, and their designs became more complex as they were embellished using embroidery or painting and dyeing techniques. Qing craftsmen repeated the legendary characters popular during the Ming period, depicting the moon goddess, the heavenly maid, the fabled 'Seven Sages of the Bamboo Grove', and the austere 'Twenty-Four Paragons of Filial Piety'. Qing textiles were dominated by a vogue for red. Because red was regarded as the colour of happiness, red tapestries were often presented on festive occasions, featuring the symbols for a happy life. A phoenix was believed to bring joy, the unicorn expressed the hope for noble sons, while the Buddhist lion was a symbol of power and valour. Deer, cranes and peaches symbolized longevity.

The 'cut silk' tapestries known as kesi are among the most valuable of all Chinese textiles. Named for the visible slits between colour breaks, the technique was practised during the Han and Tang dynasties but reached its zenith during the Song dynasty. Kesi are made through a labour-intensive weaving technique that decorates both sides of the textile, making them reversible for use as hanging screens or room dividers. Kesi often depict figures with their features drawn in ink rather than woven or embroidered.

Chinese batik fabrics are also reversible, and hung as screens, curtains and wall coverings. Since ancient times, batik prints have been created by using a resist-dyeing technique, in which designs are stamped on cotton cloth with wax, covering areas of cloth that are not to be dyed. Further layers of wax are added or removed prior to immersing the cloth in other colours of dye. The most beautiful batiks in China are those painted by the tribal Miao people.

Silk banners embroidered in gold and silver thread decorated the home with characters and motifs that conveyed good wishes and welcoming greetings. The banners could be fixed to the walls like scrolls for everyday decoration or they could be hung overhead during festivities.

Silk flags were also hung from above or flown outside, usually as a means of denoting the rank of government officials. Flags were embroidered with blazing red suns, five-toed dragons and a range of symbols and animals. Thousands were produced over the years and, like sleeve bands and textile remnants, these are easily found today in vintage textile boutiques or from antique dealers. The graphic quality of their emblems and symbols brings colour to any interior, whether framed on a wall or flown overhead.

For centuries European craftsmen were unable to rival the intricate stitching for which Chinese needlework was renowned, and magnificent silk embroideries were often displayed in the extravagant interiors of the Baroque period. Chinese embroidered wall hangings depicted genre scenes, deities and elements of the natural world with stunning expression – the vivid colour palette they created was unparalleled in the West. In the silk wall hanging shown here, two pheasants perch in a forest glade where exquisite roses bloom alongside a tranquil pool.

Embroidery

'Fine feathers make fine birds', proclaims one ancient Chinese maxim, to highlight the importance of refined detailing in decorative works. Applied to fabrics, this declaration describes the place that works of embroidery hold in the traditional Chinese home, where they embellish household items, furniture, wall hangings and articles of clothing with delicate pastels, rich jewel colours and spectacular motifs. In early centuries the fine stitching and intricate details displayed in Chinese embroidery were revered throughout the ancient world, until they were eclipsed by the silk trade. For centuries afterwards, embroidery was regarded as purely a domestic pastime, though many examples of fine needlework were traded along the Silk Route and shipped to the West via textile merchants in Canton.

In China, embroidery even adorned items made for everyday use. Cases made to hold chopsticks, scissors, knives and sets of scales were richly embroidered, as were small receptacles for fans, eyeglasses and money. Household goods like curtains, quilts, tablecloths and pillowcases were often stitched with motifs and decorations, while clothing and accessories were equipped with detachable cuffs and collars crafted from embroidered velvets and silks. Elaborate appliqué borders ornamented both robes and bedding, along with gold braiding and round silk cords made to edge the most elaborate textiles. The Chinese term for this type of trim carries the same meaning as the words for decorative fretwork or railings, making it clear that it was viewed as an integral part of the overall fabric and not merely a decorative afterthought.

The embroidered fabrics prepared for a wedding dowry would furnish the home for generations. Curtains and valances were made not just for windows but also for doors, while pillow covers were made for sets of bedding and soft cushions for the reception rooms. The bride was delivered to her husband's family in a sedan chair along with her embroidered treasures, which included three pairs of silk shoes that she was obliged to make for her new husband and his father and mother. These objects demonstrated the bride's best needlework skills as a means of proving her worth to her husband and his family, showing her usefulness to the household and her willingness to perform the most menial of tasks.

The leisure time of wealthy Chinese families was often spent in industrious activities regarded as cultural pursuits. Men occupied themselves with the scholarly arts while women devoted a large part of their time to making embroideries and decorating textiles. They often based embroideries on the best paintings in the family's collection, creating a type of work now referred to as 'the embroidery of the inner chambers'. This genre takes its name from the rooms in a Chinese home set aside for the exclusive use of the household's women, where they spent their working hours and often their leisure time. Here stitching techniques were passed down from mother to daughter, along with the patterns of classical motifs. Like the images of butterflies sipping nectar from peonies that symbolized a lover tasting the joys of passion, the significance of each motif took on a variety of meanings. Other designs depicted courtly ladies in gardens or on moonlit terraces, surrounded by birds and insects, animals, trees and flowers. Chinese women viewed their embroidery as a source of pride and self-esteem, many regarding it as their biggest achievement, apart from bearing sons.

Brocades have been prominent in Chinese textiles since ancient times. The best silk brocades employed gold or silver threads to create the raised figures and motifs characteristic of this technique. These were accentuated by other colours, or were crafted in bold relief by wrapping a fine filament of gold and silver foil around a silk thread. Metallic threads are less commonly used today; although this dragon's head has the luminosity of silver, its form is stitched into the fabric using strands of shimmering silk.

During the Ming and Qing dynasties the domestic art of embroidery was transformed into an industry that existed outside the home. Embroideries were bought by the wealthy to decorate their interiors or present to temples and monasteries as tokens of religious devotion. By the late Qing period the embroidery trade had evolved into a commercial market that continued to produce prestige items for the wealthy, while making everyday items that could be purchased for modest sums. Embroidery shops specialized in goods for the interior, selling the same kind of items as were traditionally presented by a bride to her new family. Brocades also gained currency within this industry, with those featuring raised figures in gold or silver threads especially prized by the Qing court.

Chinese embroideries are renowned for their floral motifs. These can appear in simple outline but are usually stitched from viewpoints that mimic a three-dimensional perspective to make the blooms and foliage more stylized or naturalistic in appearance. Usually they depict as blossoming flowers maturing on climbing vines, or the gentle droop of peonies, azaleas and morning glories. Floral motifs often include other elements from the natural world, depicting rolling waves, scrolling clouds, tropical fruits, butterflies and exotic birds perched on trailing branches. These embroideries adorn household textiles as well as robes, banners and ritual artefacts.

The intricate stitching and exquisite details of sleeve bands have always made them attractive features, whether attached to clothing or not. Certain types of sleeve band were designed with motifs stitched vertically so that they could be viewed as upright images when the wearer folded their arms in front of them. These were often embroidered with characters that illustrated a story told in literature or poetry, or depicted themes ranging from the four seasons to the five virtues. Sleeve bands share characteristics common to tapestries, giving them the feel of miniature tapestries when used as wall hangings. Hanging scrolls were made of similar embroidered silks but were considerably wider and longer.

Imperial Dress

When the Manchus conquered China in 1644 their robes were a hybrid of their own dress and that of the Chinese. As they rose to power they adopted the embroidered sleeve ends of Chinese robes, creating full cuffs with elaborate detailing. Dress in imperial China was always highly codified, with the decorative motifs of court costumes and officials' robes strictly designated by rank. Among the emblems reserved for the emperor's robes were the twelve imperial symbols of the sun, the moon and the constellations; mountains, water and fire; birds, weed and millet, cups and axes, the auspicious *fu* symbol and nine five-clawed dragons. The emperor's dragon robe was worn during religious festivals and periods of fasting – except for a few details in black, white and pale blue, the dragon robe was embroidered in fine gold and silver threads. As well as the standard imperial symbols, the emperor's dragon robe featured clouds, waves and rocky promontories that were symmetrically arranged to represent the order of the cosmos.

As the dragon was the principal motif embroidered on court robes, its poses and styles were varied and complex. The number of dragons allowed on any one garment was an important signifier of the wearer's status. All differences in material, colour and cut of the robes were determined by imperial codes and protocols. At the time of the last Qing emperors, dragon robes were full-length with side fastenings, and structured more like overcoats than loose robes. Dragon robes were also worn by the empress and the women of the imperial household, as well as the wives of the senior officials entitled to wear them. Apart from dragon robes, and needlework roundels on garments, it was unusual for Chinese men to wear embroidered clothing. Embroidered floral motifs, butterflies and garden scenes were more typical of women's robes, while men's robes were usually decorated by patterns woven into the silk on the loom.

The robes of other court officials were embellished with emblems and badges of rank, worn to signify the difference between officials and the wealthy courtiers who were not in service to the emperor. Rank badges were square in shape, often with dark blue backgrounds, and embroidered with a variety of birds, animals or mythological creatures, each symbolizing a different rank within the imperial hierarchy. Protocols in the Ming and Qing dynasties stipulated that a civil official's rank should be a bird: for example, a red-crowned crane, oriole, quail or goose. Animal designs were allocated to military officers, who wore tigers, rhinoceros, leopards and brown bears. The meaning of the emblems changed between the dynasties and rulers as the animals took on new cultural meanings over time.

Sleeve bands were sewn onto robes as cuffs, joined to the fabric at the wrist or elongated to cover the hands as a sign that the wearer did not perform menial tasks. These were generally made in light pastel colours or creams, probably to contrast with the darker background of the robe itself. Because light colours were reserved for mourning, it is unusual to find robes with white backgrounds, even among those made especially for export to the West. Though human figures were rarely embroidered onto the robe itself, sleeve bands depicted warriors and legendary characters from literature and poetry along with deities and the Chinese Immortals. Often the stitching is so fine it is virtually invisible, and the colours so rich that they continue to look vibrant today.

This magnificent robe is indicative of the Manchu imperial style, embroidered with the five-clawed dragon, one of the twelve symbols of imperial sovereignty used in China since the Han dynasty. At the bottom of the robe, representations of invisible cosmic rays and turbulent waves encircle the wearer, along with the other-worldly forms the Chinese believe to exist in the human realm. The dragons move amidst scrolling clouds, with a radiating sun or glowing moon in their centre. The embroidered sleeve bands are shaped in a horse's hoof design and feature miniature versions of the motifs decorating the front and back of the robe.

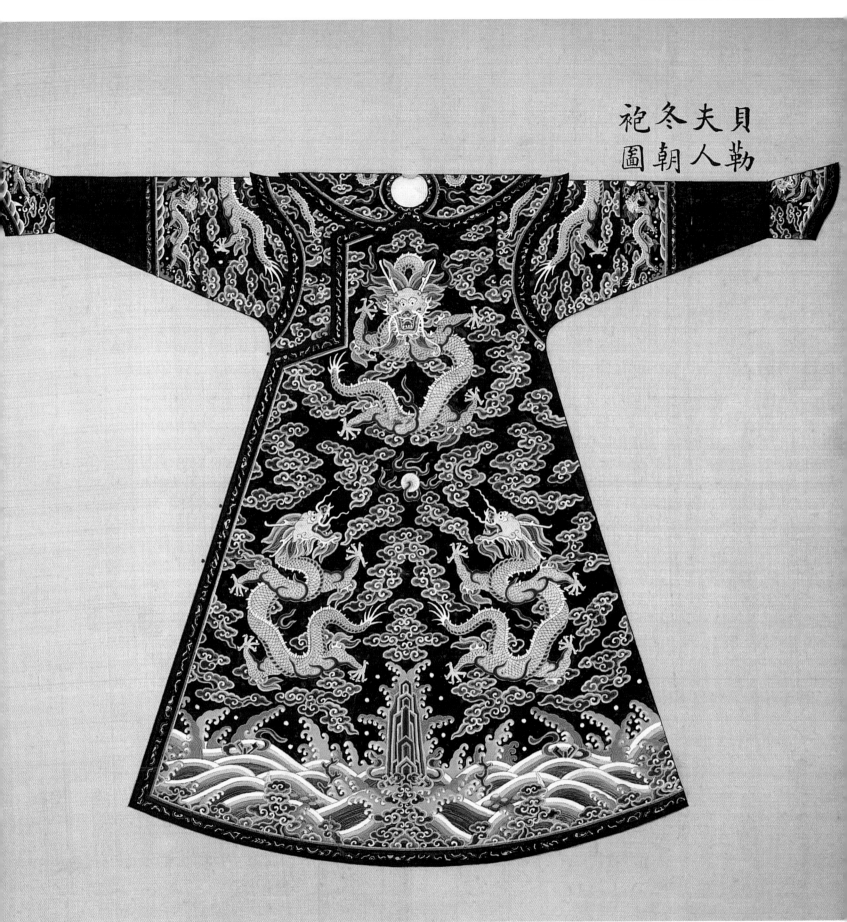

袍冬夫貝
圖朝人勒

DECORATIVE DETAILS

裝飾細節

DECORATIVE DETAILS

Throughout history, the emperors of China retained artists and craftsmen to produce works of subtle beauty and exquisite workmanship. One of the emperor's principal roles was that of arbiter of taste for the empire as a whole, and each dynasty created a powerful aesthetic that would distinguish it from previous dynasties. By the end of the Qing dynasty, the imperial collections had swelled to vast proportions, and thousands of artists still continued to labour in the palace workshops. Works crafted in the precious materials of jade, ivory, silver and gold were produced for the imperial household, along with paintings, portraits and cartouche to line the walls of the palaces. While each object was created to affirm the power and glory of the state and thus the legitimacy of the emperor, they also set the style for the rest of the empire.

Outside the palace, the decorative arts flourished with the support of court patrons. Many private workshops were established during the late sixteenth and early seventeenth centuries to make luxury items for the merchants and scholars living in the south of China. Craftsmen captured beauty in the most unlikely objects: boxes, utensils, cups, books made of stone tablets, scrolls, incense burners and an overwhelming array of ritual and functional items. Motifs ranged from the decorative to the symbolic, usually falling into the themes of protection, virtue, magic and immortality. Thunderclouds and scrolling clouds heralded the arrival of deities, while turbulent waves, rolling waves and cresting waves rolled mysteriously across dry land as well as the sea. Buddhist artefacts and ceremonial objects influenced the colour and design of many decorative items, juxtaposed with vernacular styles and Islamic influences from the Middle East. Calligraphy was elevated to an art form, practised on ornamental scrolls and tablets to display in the interior.

Traditionally, the Chinese preferred materials that could be worked into a smooth surface with a soft sheen, and items crafted in horn, ivory, precious wood, lacquer resin and stone were carved intricately. The Chinese love of jade is thought to explain their reluctance to cut crystalline stones for their sparkle, preferring always a smooth ground surface. The significance of stone to the Chinese went beyond its form: the slow process of working stone was likened to the onerous process of perfecting the human mind; only through long and unrelenting effort could true character and virtue be achieved. Poems extolled the soft sheen stone takes on when polished, and marvelled that it could be cool to the touch, yet warm when held in the hand. Materials like gilt, painted enamel and metalwork were polished to a rich lustre. The variety of materials and the expertise of the craftsmen from the first centuries through to the early twentieth century attest to the power and importance that the decorative arts gained in China.

China's imperial palace was the heart of an empire that, to the Chinese, was the centre of the aesthetic world. During each dynasty the imperial artists produced paintings with traditional themes such as portraiture, landscapes, still lifes and religious iconography, as well as detailed representations of political ceremonies, military conquests and imperial processions. Representations of nature were depicted in images of clouds and water, mountains, trees and rocks, and flowers such as orchids,

chrysanthemums and plum blossoms. Painters also practised independently of the palace, or painted in a scholarly manner, and they often worked in a looser, more understated style.

The Song dynasty is considered the golden age of Chinese painting. During this era painting evolved from line drawings of figures to highly sophisticated landscapes and flower-and-bird paintings. Landscape paintings have always been held in high esteem by the court and the literati, who contemplated the peaceful calm captured in the paintings of mountains, forests, fields, and gardens to find refuge from the material world. The flowers, trees, grass, stones, animals and birds depicted in the elegant flower-and-bird paintings were widely admired for their highly detailed depictions of flora. They became China's first botanical illustrations as horticulture and botany began to develop. Landscapes, portraits and flower-and-bird paintings continued to be the three main categories of Chinese painting until the contemporary period.

The simplicity of these paintings places emphasis on line, which is often regarded as the basis of all Chinese painting. This characteristic is shared with calligraphy, creating a close relationship between the two. The written character, in itself an abstract form, was of great value to the Chinese eye. The possession of both artistic technique and knowledge was an essential characteristic of the scholarly man, and calligraphy was the means by which the scholar could communicate. Writing enabled the scholar to enter the world of literature and the classics, and from there the world of the literati and the business of the court. Applying brush to silk or paper was an act of expressing skill, knowledge and personal style through the design and sweep of the characters. Using the same tools of brush and ink allowed the artists to represent nature as a concept, an abstraction in black and white.

Monochrome paintings were thought to have a subtle elegance inexpressible in any other paintings. The image resulting from the absence of colour was considered intense, purified by the mind as the essentials of line, shape and space, darkness and light were contemplated. As more scholars began to study painting, a 'literati' school emerged during the Yuan dynasty, characterized by a trend to fuse calligraphy and painting. These artists took inspiration from literature as well as from nature, forming a link between poetry and painting.

Scrolls were hung on walls to display poetry and verse written in elegant calligraphy. Chinese poetry provides a window through which we can observe the emotions that stirred the people of China throughout history. It ranges from the light-hearted to the intense, to deep, dark philosophical truths. Different regions developed distinctive styles of verse, which are divided into historical periods; all of these are categorized into four 'voices' of expression, and comprise a complex tradition that offers poets a broad range of modes for expression.

Early Chinese poetry was commonly believed to represent a rapport with the spirit world; its lines were long and rhapsodic, mingling the spiritual and the physical as they recounted the trance journeys of shamans. Poetry was also written purely in celebration of nature, sweeping across time and space to extol the magnificence of mountain, sea and forest.

Page 143 The decorative arts tradition flourished throughout China's long history. Though styles and aesthetics evolved with each era, the regard for craftsmanship and artistic excellence remained. Craftsmen captured beauty in almost every functional or ritual object, and created exquisite ornaments. This is evident in these hanging scrolls, woodblock prints, ornaments and porcelain figurines.

Right A traditional wide-sleeved Chinese robe makes a superb wall hanging; its proportions and concise cut are almost architectural in their simplicity. Even though this is not a ceremonial robe, the embroidered butterflies and flowers give it an elegant feel. The robe is supported by a bamboo pole pushed through the sleeves and shoulders, then fastened to the wall on both sides.

Music in China can be traced back to distant antiquity. At the time that European music was first coming to life, sophisticated musical instruments and musical theory began appearing in China as a result of the ritual music advocated by Confucius. In the cultural model that the Confucian school laid down, music was considered an integral part of the ceremonial and ritual practices connected with religious rites and ancestor worship – essentially a link between heaven and earth.

From the Han dynasty to the Qing dynasty, court music was played during banquets, ceremonies and dance performances. Court music was much more cosmopolitan than the music played for formal rituals, as it was also influenced by folk songs and music from India and Korea.

The court music of the Qing dynasty included *kunqu* opera, which the scholarly class considered to be the apogee of the dramatic arts. Traditionally *kunqu* was performed in temples, teahouses and private homes, where lattice screens formed the backdrop to the 'stage', and tables and chairs were the only props. This established a tradition for minimal set designs, and today *kunqu* continues to be performed against a simple backdrop, with a set that includes only a table and chairs. The table might symbolize an official's desk, a dining table, a bridge or even a hill.

Jingju or *jingxi*, which is known to Westerners as the Beijing or Peking opera, is a combination of regional opera styles recognized two hundred years ago by the imperial court and performed in the Mandarin language of the Qing dynasty. The Beijing opera is stylized and abstract, with the lyrics sung in a characteristic pitch that rolls the words liltingly. Cantonese opera is the standard in Hong Kong and the south, and sung rhythmically and poetically.

Above left Tang burial customs dictated that ceramic replicas of animals, people and material possessions be entombed with the dead. These two figures may have been family members or servants intended to serve the deceased in the afterlife.

Above right Lacquerware featured patterns carved into the surface of the lacquer. Here, a bat delineates the rounded handle of a serving ladle.

The singers are always dramatic – the characters become literally larger than life with platform soles, headdresses and hair ornaments that are high and almost architectural in shape. The costumes are based on the style of dress worn four centuries ago during the Ming dynasty, with exaggerated motifs that are ornamented by pennants and badges. Costumes are always colourful and resplendently embroidered, with long, flowing sleeves that trail beyond the feet, bursting into a range of fluttering and waving movements as the singers use them to express emotions. The opera singers, who train their hands to be as expressive as their face or voice, are able to articulate the full spectrum of emotions through hundreds of different hand movements, each one signalling a specific mood. Like the face make-up that creates a mask for each character, the costumes identify the character wearing them.

Gestures and symbols are used to tell the story: performers imitate men on horseback by cantering across the stage as if they were sitting in the saddle, or paddle the air rhythmically to convey a voyage across the ocean. A long stretch of time is expressed by a slow saunter around the stage. In dances, sleeves, fans, and collared satin ribbons are transformed into weapons or tools, and embodied with rich theatrical meaning.

Cross-dressing has characterized Chinese opera for centuries. Beijing opera rarely has female performers, as all the women are traditionally played by men. The most famous opera diva was a man, Mei Lanfang, who became a cultural icon in the early 1900s; his opera roles set the ideal of feminine style and beauty for two generations. At the turn of the last century Mei performed in Europe and in the United States to worldwide acclaim.

Opposite The gentle curves of a stylized Buddha are enveloped within the folds of his robe as he sits in meditation atop a sideboard. Traditionally he would have been placed in the centre of the household shrine as the central focus of religious practice. Today the dignity and serenity of the Buddha introduces the same element of calm to any interior.

Craftsmanship

During the Xia, Shang and Qin dynasties, as the early rulers of northern China forged trade links with the eastern Mediterranean, the Middle East and Central Asia, Chinese craftsmen were influenced by new and different decorative styles and techniques. The shapes and methods that were introduced were adapted to suit Chinese tastes, and traditional Chinese ceremonial and luxury objects began to show signs of Islamic, Ottoman, Persian and Greek design.

Silver and goldsmithing techniques were developed by the Chinese during the Tang dynasty. However, a native tradition in silversmithing was not established until the Song dynasty, and it never achieved the sophistication of design and craftsmanship accomplished in works of gold. Gold and silver became popular again during the Yuan dynasty, with new forms and motifs resulting from the influence of the Middle East, but these were mostly works made for the imperial household and the Buddhist temples patronized by the nobility.

By the Han period, bronze was considered rare and precious by the ancient Chinese, who often preferred it to silver and gold. They used bronze to cast large quantities of ritual vessels, weapons and a range of musical instruments that were elegant in form, finely decorated, and inscribed with calligraphy or auspicious motifs. Bronze was also crafted into vases, food dishes and vessels for wine and water. Endless variation is found in both the form and the design of these early pieces, fully demonstrating the rich imagination, creativity and craft techniques of the first Chinese artisans. Dishes and platters for food were cast in many different styles, with scalloped rims and lobed outlines. Vessels for water were generally cast with a circular base to stabilize the belly, while others had a heavy square base added onto the rounded belly to create a dramatic contrast of geometrical forms. Wine vessels were designed so that they could be heated and poured from a single container. Pour spouts and side handles enabled them to be easily decanted, and the tripod base allowed it to be placed directly onto the coals.

Bronze vessels were widely used in banquets and ceremonies held in palaces and temples, and as funerary items for deceased nobility. They featured inlaid patterns in silver, gold, copper and turquoise, crafted into interlocking geometrical shapes based on straight lines and diagonals, or whorled lines and spirals. They also featured motifs depicting animals, dragons, flowers and butterflies. Emperors inscribed vessels with verses honouring the ministers and nobility who made great contributions to the nation or to the sovereign, in order to establish a lasting record for later generations to read.

Incense burners were first cast in bronze during the early Shang and Zhou dynasties, in shapes so refined that they became design classics, repeated for several thousand years. Many of the incense burners made in the Ming and Qing dynasties had finishes to make them resemble the original artefact. Great skill was used to create patinations of rich auburn and tea green, dashed with gold and gilded by fire. This technique suspended the gold in a mercury amalgam and applied it to the bronze; when heated, the mercury ran off the surface, leaving a marbled effect on the incense burner.

Cloisonné was created through firing techniques that fused coloured enamels to the surface of a copper or bronze object. A rudimentary form of cloisonné was introduced to China from the Middle East during the Yuan dynasty, and was perfected as a result of the technical skills of Chinese artisans. The imperial workshops had already developed sophisticated metallurgical technology to cast bronze and ceramics, and glaze production techniques were well advanced.

Rich patterns and illustrations could be created by the cloisonné enamels as they were inlaid among brass or copper wires soldered to the surface of the objects. As the ground enamels melted into the metal, the colours took on a high gloss, and the wires running between them kept them neatly separated. Once they cooled, the wires were polished to a high sheen, giving the appearance of tiny veins of gold threaded through the intricate patterns. More luxurious items had gold plating applied to the wires, the rim and the bottom surface, creating an object that appeared to be made of glass and gold. Cloisonné greatly appealed to Chinese sensibilities – the enamel was as smooth and lustrous as jade, yet glittered like jewellery.

Bronze was a favourite of craftsmen because of its durability and the ease with which it could be cast. From ancient times, a variety of tools, utensils and cookware have been cast in bronze, and many of the 'name chops' used by the Chinese throughout the centuries were cast in bronze. From official government papers to private contracts, all business and civil transactions require both a signature and the stamp of the name chop to be legally binding. Each name chop is individually designed, combining the beauty of calligraphy with an individual motif set within a 1cm (½in) square stamp, sometimes also made of stone. Craftsmen, calligraphers and painters stamp their works with their name chops to 'sign' them and provide proof of their authenticity. As the name chop reproduces the same image again and again, it is thought to be a forerunner of Chinese printing.

The skill required to craft ivory went beyond the ability to engrave motifs and carve likenesses; the demand for it in both China and the West called for expertise more advanced than that of many other craft traditions. Even as early as the Song dynasty, ivory was polychromed and gilded, and often more finely detailed than the bronze, wood and stone sculptures made at the time. The development of Buddhist thought in China created a market for images that paid homage to the Buddha and his bodhisattvas, which merged Indian influences with existing Taoist styles. In the late Ming dynasty, Canton had close ties to the Philippines, which had been conquered by the Spanish. The Spaniards, like other Europeans with settlements in the Orient, began to commission devotional figures carved in ivory to decorate their churches in the East.

Chinese ivory figures are primarily representations of divinities, be they influenced by Buddhist, Taoist, Christian or Hindu deities. Other types of figures are usually decorated plaques and ornamental objects, carved in high relief to emphasize the intricate details of their robes and jewellery. Elaborate objects like musical instruments and folding fans were made by craftsmen with special technical skills, while simple articles like brush holders, wrist rests, round boxes and handles could easily be produced in mass quantities. Canton became a second centre for ivory when craftsmen trained in the Qing workshops were relocated to have better access to the material. All ivory was imported from overseas, some coming from as far away as Africa. Although climatic changes caused the elephant to become extinct in China two thousand years ago, it did not interrupt the production of ivory goods, which has continued unabated ever since.

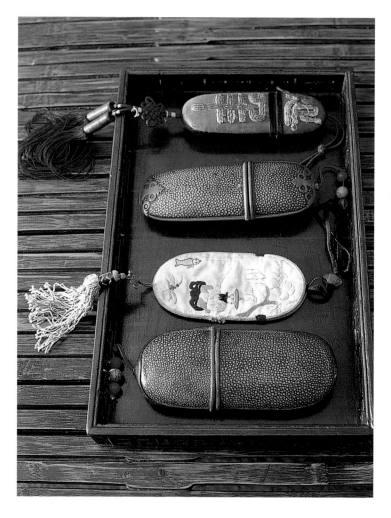

Above left
Ink sticks and ink stones are among many functional objects that have been appropriated for their decorative value today.

Above right Small cases, such as these spectacles cases, were made from a range of materials, including embroidered silk, tortoiseshell, ivory, horn and metal. Fitted with tassels and handles, they could be carried like a small handbag or tucked deep inside a sleeve and easily extracted by pulling the tassel.

Opposite Chinese papercuts are a traditional folk art that dates back more than 1,500 years. Crafted from tissue-thin rice paper and hand-painted with Chinese ink, each motif is a continuous piece cut into a variety of shapes and figures. The framed papercuts here create a colourful display of flowers, patterns and mythological figures.

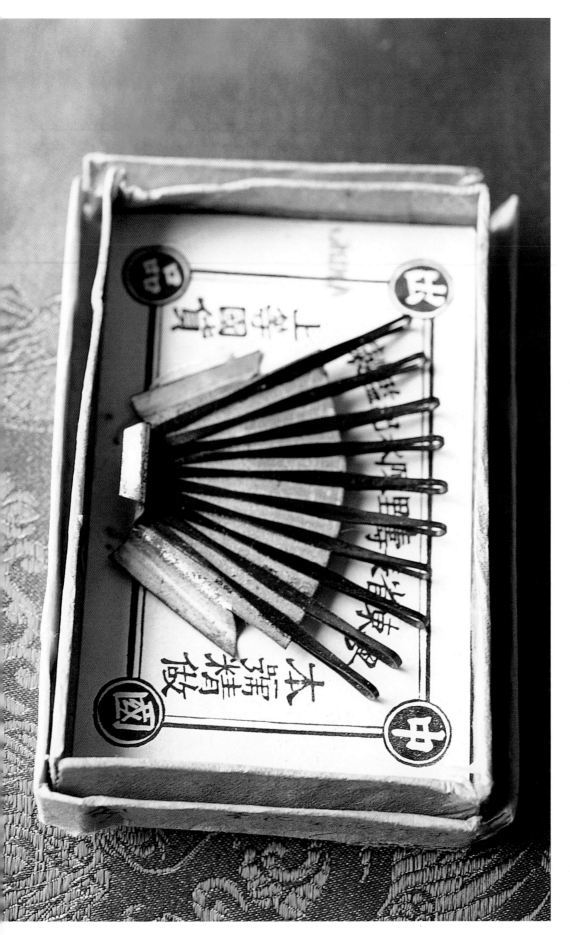

Left Hairgrips like these were essential to create the elaborate hair styles of Chinese women, such as the coiffure worn by the Dowager Empress on page 43. For the Empress, however, hairgrips of jade or precious metals would have been used instead of these factory-made ones.

Opposite Porcelain figurines like these were produced as chinoiserie exports by the ceramic factories of Canton, where they would have been fired by the hundreds. Their style of dress indicates that they may be children or performing artists, and the pose they sit in suggests that they are seated on low three-legged stools, as was the practice throughout most of southern China.

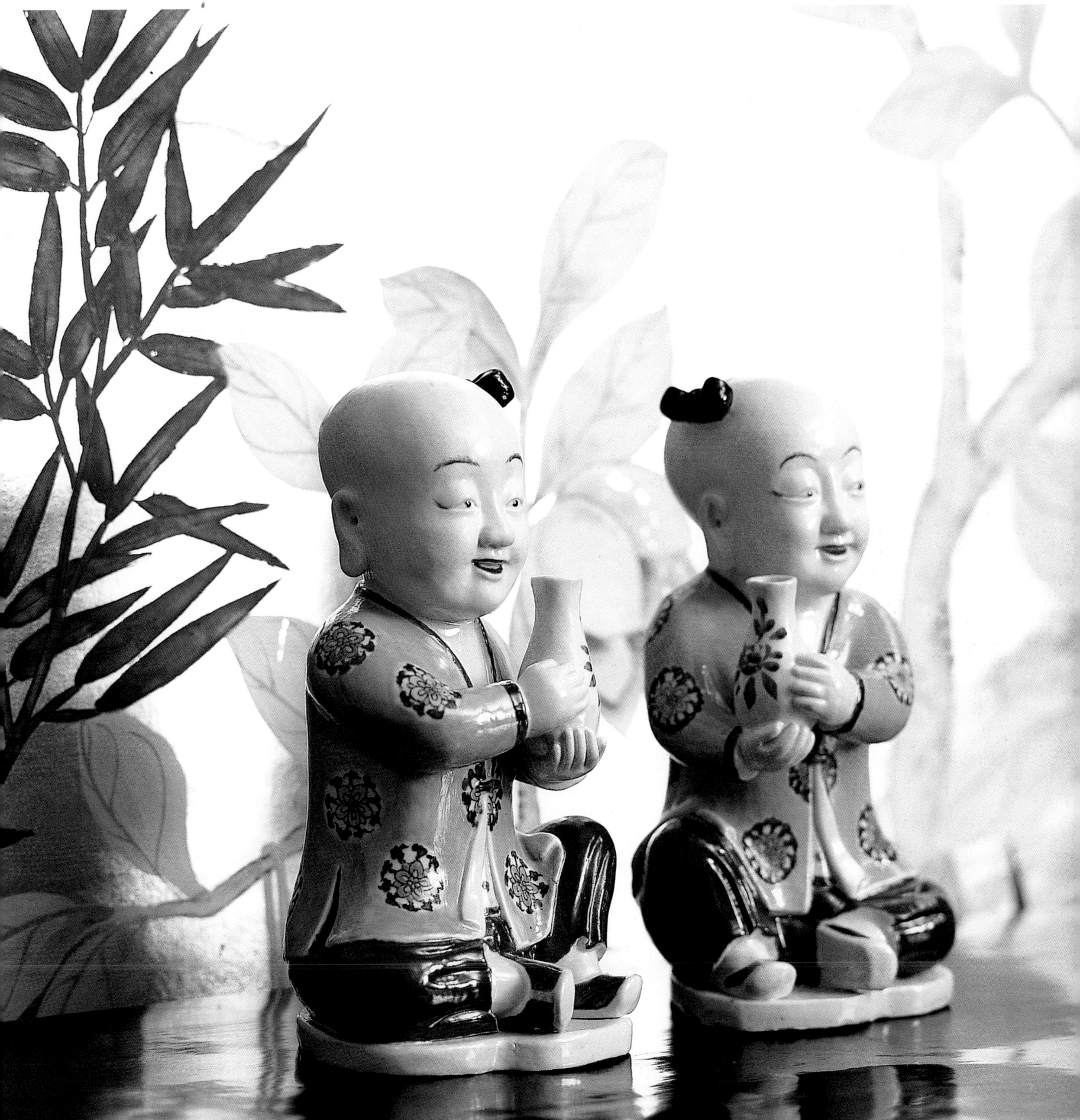

Lacquerware

The lustrous beauty of lacquer and the sophisticated techniques applied to crafting it give lacquered objects a look of luxury. With this in mind, the Chinese coated almost everything imaginable with lacquer to endow it with beauty and value. Musical instruments, writing tools, bowls and utensils for eating and drinking, furniture, funerary objects, weapons and even transportation vehicles were coated in lacquer. Pictures and patterns were carved into the surface of the lacquer, depicting dragons, phoenixes, lotus ponds, waterfowl and other elements of the natural world. Platters, bowls, boxes and furnishings were adorned with festive scenes or depicted fierce warriors, serene deities, groups of children, courtly ladies and huntsmen.

Lacquerware paralleled many articles originally made in the ceramic workshops, imitating the scalloped rims and raised edges of banquet platters and everyday dishes. Ritual objects like incense boxes, three-dimensional cosmic diagrams known as mandalas, ceremonial rice measures and figures of deities were also made in the lacquer workshops for shrines in the temple as well as the home. Lacquered chests and cabinets were sometimes made to create the illusion of several ornate boxes casually stacked together, or several boxes held together by gilt handles mounted as though they could be easily carried away. Real lacquer boxes could be made with compartments to contain delicacies for a picnic, or for use by the scholar to carry scrolls, brushes and inks. Lacquer boxes fitted with basketry panels were used for the presentation of gifts and documents, or as a decorative means of storage in the home.

When lacquered boxes, chests and platters were chosen as gifts, the motifs adorning them were also selected to convey the sentiments appropriate for the occasion. Images of ritual objects like water ewers, incense boxes and grain vessels could be combined with prosperity symbols, such as moulds for minting coins, to create subtle messages. The name for a grain vessel, *fu*, and a coin, *qian*, would form the basis of the expression *fuzai yangqian*, meaning 'happiness is right here'. When the gift was presented, the good wishes expressed in the motif were offered as well.

A style of carved lacquer known as *tixi*, which became popular during the Song dynasty and remained in vogue through the Yuan and Ming dynasties, is characterized by decorative patterns and scenes that are carved in either red or black lacquer. Thin layers of black were applied between the coatings of red – or vice versa – subtly deepening the tone. This effect worked especially well in relief because it enhanced the illusion of depth and foreground that artists used to create several distinct scenes within a flat surface. The motifs found on *tixi* wares are more robust than the delicate works of later centuries; they are charged with a vitality that makes them unique among Chinese lacquerware.

During the Qing dynasty, the development of a moulding technique made it possible to cast figures and ornaments in solid lacquer. This gave the industry tremendous commercial potential, but many of the Chinese eschewed the thought of lacquerware multiples. Most of these were eventually made for export, being early versions of the moulded plastic objects that would make the 'Made in China' sticker an emblem of China in later centuries.

Opposite Lacquer is enjoying a revival as leading designers apply traditional lacquer techniques to new forms. Here, the Chinese-American designer Robert Kuo has crafted a nest of lacquered copper bowls inspired by organic shapes.

Page 156 The Chinese coated a vast range of objects with lacquer to heighten their aesthetic appeal and practicality. Small lacquerware containers (top left) were used to store food, as their lacquered finishes created a watertight surface. These bowls (top right) combine traditional lacquer techniques with early metal-casting methods, using copper to craft these bowls and lacquer to decorate them. A simple bowl (bottom left) is transformed by two contrasting lacquer finishes, and a contemporary lacquerware tray (bottom right) is juxtaposed against an older classic behind it. *Page 157* This collection of modern and vintage pieces illustrates the timeless appeal of lacquered finishes. Antique porcelain, vintage hairgrips, and modern plastic and glass stand on a lacquered surface.

Jade & Precious Stones

Though jade may appear to be merely a beautiful stone with a lustrous green colour, to the Chinese it is 'the essence of heaven and earth'. Jade is found in mountains and riverbeds, places Chinese consider to be sacred and brimming with auspicious *qi*. This is why jade has long been a potent symbol of vitality, protection and immortality throughout Chinese history. It was so popular in ancient times that by 1500 BC some native sources of jade in China began to be depleted, and the stone had to be imported from sources in central Asia and Burma that were thousands of miles away.

Of the semi-precious stones that the Chinese identify as jade, only two are recognized by modern geologists as true jade. Jadeite, which is native to Burma, is bright green, and nephrite, which is found near the ancient cities of Khotan and Yarkand in Central Asia, comes in many shades of green, yellow and translucent white. Both stones contain finely variegated colours that lend a sense of texture and patina beneath their soft sheen.

Jade articles were initially crafted as emblems of supernatural and temporal powers. The stone was worked into ceremonial vessels, weapons and talismans by some of China's earliest Neolithic cultures, before becoming widely used for jewellery, furnishings, figures and ornaments. Imperial orders and medallions were crafted in jade and given to the nobility as symbols of their office or authority. When the emperor dispatched a prince, or other high-ranking mandarin for official duty, he might have been given a jade tablet proclaiming the 'divine orders' assigned to him by the ruling 'son of heaven'.

As jade became a part of the decorative arts movement that flourished in China during the late sixteenth and early seventeenth centuries, it was crafted into luxury items for scholars and mandarins living in southern China. Such items included brush holders, brush washers, books, small sculptures, wine cups and chimes. Women wore combs, hairpins, bracelets and waist pendants crafted in jade, and they embroidered jade ornaments into their robes, sashes and caps. Each piece exhibited delicate detailing and exquisite workmanship, reflecting the high quality of life aspired to by the Chinese.

At the time of the Emperor Qianlong, who reigned from 1736 to 1796, the imperial workshops made luxury items in amber, agate, lapis lazuli, turquoise, soapstone and malachite, which were often crafted by artisans who had worked in jade. Lapis lazuli and malachite were prized for their veins of blue and green that evoked the tones of jade, and both minerals were ground into pigments for painting.

Amber was also widely used in China during the Tang dynasty, when magical properties were sometimes ascribed to it. Tang scholars identified how its formation occurred over many centuries, and noted that amber occasionally contained embedded insects. Jewellery and furniture inlays were its most popular uses, but it was also carved into small sculptures and figurines.

Soapstone can resemble the golden tones of amber, but while amber has reddish accents, soapstone's accents verge towards brown and it rarely has the translucency of amber. Even so, soapstone could be crafted into beautifully variegated sculptures. Its dense grain made it an ideal representation of a mountain or rock, and it was often used to depict them in sculptures and inlays.

Revered by the Chinese since Neolithic times, jade became more commonplace throughout the decorative arts of the late sixteenth and early seventeenth centuries. When the Han dynasty craftsmen created this jade head and torso, jade was believed to be imbued with supernatural powers that conferred protection and longevity.

Fans

The fans of imperial China were not only artistic fashion accessories that provided protection from the sun and shielded the face from unwelcome gazes. Fans were also used to intensify the heat of a fire in a stove or brazier, or were fixed to the ceiling to cool the interior during the hot summer. This type of overhanging fan, similar to the Indian *punkah*, is made of cloth or sometimes reed or rattan and became known in southern China as the *chuke*. It was pulled back and forth by strings attached to two floorboards and operated by moving the feet in a pedalling motion. This early version of a ceiling fan was used until the twentieth century, when it was replaced by the electric fan.

Though fans originated as functional items, over time they became a medium for artistic expression, and often bore scenes and motifs painted onto their leaves or the mounts to which they were secured. When these were decorated by well-known painters or exchanged as tokens of friendship, their owners carefully removed them from their mounts and fixed them to individual sheets of paper to preserve them. Fan leaves painted by famous artists were so treasured that they were positioned on album pages, framed and hung on the wall, or fastened to hanging scrolls and fixed to the falls. Fan paintings may feature a bird-and-flower motif, a landscape or pastoral scene, figures, animals or calligraphy. Fans also had significance when captured in portraits. They would denote the status and sensibilities of the portrait sitters, or add a subtle emotive note to the image of women featured in paintings by the way in which they were gesturing with their fans.

The first fans of fashion were invented by the Chinese, and are believed to have emerged in the early Han dynasty. These were typically made with a silk face stretched over a rounded bamboo frame, which was mounted on a long-stemmed handle. During the Tang dynasty, artists and scholars were encouraged to demonstrate their writing and painting skills by using fan faces as a medium. The Tang literati gave fans considerable social significance and made them a standard part of the summer costume worn by the scholarly and the elite.

Feather fans were made from all types of bird's feather, ranging from the exotic peacock to the ordinary chicken. Goose feathers were a particular favourite, but feathers from pheasants, falcons, cranes and hawks were considered more stylish choices. Hair fans made from the tails of horses and deer were popular during the Han dynasty and were better suited to chasing away unwelcome insects than stirring up a cool breeze. They resembled feather dusters more than typical fans, and were used by officials and noblemen as status symbols. Members of the ruling class were often painted with hair fans in their hands to denote their rank, even in later dynasties.

Folding fans were probably introduced to China from Japan or Korea during the Song dynasty, yet did not achieve widespread popularity until the Ming years. The faces were usually made from fine paper mounted onto thin ribs of bamboo pinned together in a flexible, tier-like structure. Like the fixed fans, these were highly decorated by artists and the literati. The folding fan led in popularity from then until the nineteenth century, when the round fan made a mild comeback. At that time, there was also a vogue for fixing them to walls and furniture as decorative artworks.

Folding fans date back to the Song dynasty, yet were not fully embraced as fashion accessories until the Ming period. The folding fan then led in popularity until the nineteenth century, when the unbendable round fan made a comeback. Embroidered cases like these were made to store the fans when not in use. They remained popular even when folding fans went out of vogue, as they were put to use as holders for chopsticks, scissors and letter openers.

Display

Chinese style is seductive – real enthusiasts often let their passion for Chinese decor take over their living space, colour themes, art collection and choice of furniture. And why not? Chinese art pieces and craftworks bring with them a rich heritage of design and timeless materials that can add colour and exoticism to any interior, without necessarily transforming it into a shrine to Chinese culture.

Often in the West a room is decorated to emphasize the main features, with the decorative details chosen merely to enhance them. The patterns, pictures, ornaments and artefacts adorning the rooms in which the Chinese live and work are carefully considered for their craftsmanship and special qualities. Each object is chosen to convey family values, status, power and spirituality. Colour, whether lavishly used or somewhat understated, is considered in relation to ornaments and artwork, to create a harmony of tone and colour in the interior that give it a sense of completeness. The variety of decorative elements drawn together are recognized by the Chinese as a genre in its own right – the art of the interior.

The art decorating a Chinese home has been chosen not only for its beauty, but also for its references to scholarly knowledge and spiritual awakening. It is often considered to be in effect a portrait of the owners, reflecting their tastes in classicism, their eye for balance, their appreciation of craftsmanship and their regard for the natural world. In previous centuries this reflected the approach of the Chinese scholar, who included art as part of a theoretical and spiritual education. Wealthy mandarins would retire after a short career and devote their fortune to the artistic pursuits of an elegant life, refining the interiors of their homes through collections of art and artefacts, or creating a contemplative garden.

Today, the trend for minimal living and the influence of feng shui has created a modern ethos of living without clutter that recalls the simplicity of the Ming dynasty. Surfaces can be kept bare – as they were then – by confining *objets d'art* to display cabinets or open shelves, or recessing them into a wall niche.

Chinese paintings and hanging scrolls provide the ultimate backdrop to Chinese-inspired collections, as well as filling the interior with beautiful images. These set the tone of the room if they are hung over the mantelpiece or are positioned to be the first thing that is seen when entering a room. The Chinese usually hang scrolls and paintings in pairs or in serried ranks along the walls, sometimes at table height where they can be read at eye level when sitting down. Stone tablets, plaques or antique medallions also make interesting wall hangings, and create a sense of the history behind the millennia of Chinese style.

Every available surface can be appropriated as a display area. Scale is an important consideration – small items like name chops (see page 149), snuff boxes (which can look more like tiny porcelain bottles) and ink stones (see page 168) tend to get lost on a broad surface and are better suited to smaller spaces. For an effective display, combinations of varying heights and contrasting shapes can be grouped together according to similarities in style, function, colour or even period. That said, it can be even more effective to display two or three figures that really stand out, rather than hiding them among a number of less interesting figures.

Opposite A collection of early twentieth-century posters creates an arresting single display.

Page 164 The circular shape of a contemporary lacquerware platter provides an antidote to the sharp angles of a minimal interior. Contoured pieces soften harsh lines: here the rounded lacquerware erases the symmetry of the parallel lines, while the mother-of-pearl mobile above it diffuses the low edges created by the 'floating' ceiling.

Page 165 The irregular shapes provided by a lacquered fretwork screen create the perfect setting for small objects – both front and back are made immediately visible. These late nineteenth-century snuff bottles are made from glass and rock crystal.

Calligraphy

Calligraphy, 'the art of writing', turns a word into a picture, captured in the measured sweep of brush and ink. The meanings contained in each character form a sentence or tell a story, transforming an entire text into a readable work of art. The Chinese alphabet is so rich in imagery that the style of the calligrapher can illustrate the meaning of the story as lavishly as a picture. The calligrapher's brush can also create austere black-and-white landscapes; many generations of artists have used it to translate nature into ink.

The essence of calligraphy lies in its relationship to the Chinese decorative arts. Calligraphy combines the intellectual beauty of what the words mean with the visual beauty of how the words are written. The Chinese believe that written words have mystic meanings, and their calligraphic representations are regarded as magical symbols for health, happiness, wealth or good fortune. These characters feature in the motifs decorating furniture, ceramics, woodwork and textiles, to invoke the protection of the spirit world and sanctify the household and its visitors. So great is their power that the ancients would sit in contemplation of the characters. Like a dreamer awakened, a new sense of the words would unfold, giving insight into their mystic meanings.

Calligraphy is also written to be mounted on decorative scrolls and hung prominently in the formal rooms to greet visitors with messages of good wishes or poetic verse. Carved wooden plaques or stone tablets are etched with Buddhist scriptures or references to countless generations of ancestors. Often crafted from ebony, jade, mother-of-pearl or rich lacquerwork, with the characters outlined in gold leaf or gold powder, these are revered as precious artworks.

The calligrapher works at a writing table, sitting and contemplating the movement of the brush and the surface of the paper before drawing. Getting the feel of the paper is part of the process – he handles the paper and studies its surface, examining its texture and porosity before laying it flat on the table. Identification with the materials is an essential tenet of Taoism and Confucianism, as it is believed to facilitate the expression of spiritual awakening in the act of creation. The calligrapher waits for the *qi* to rise through the body, believing this to be the inspiration behind what is to be transmitted to the paper. A calligrapher sees himself or herself as a tool, not the source, with the brush a conduit for the mysteries of creation.

A topic debated by artists and scholars alike is the merits of various inks. A deep, glossy black ink wash is traditionally based on resinous pine soot and binding gum, mixed inside a deep metal mortar and pounded together with a heavy pestle. Musk, camphor and other fragrances are added to the mixture to mask the odour of the gum just before the ink paste is pressed into wooden moulds. Once the ink cakes set, they are elaborately decorated with symbols or motifs by skilled craftsmen. In the hands of the calligrapher, they are gently rubbed against the coarse surface of an ink stone, which dissolves them into fine powder.

At this stage, water is added, but it has to be done drop by drop, to avoid the extremes of 'too wet' or 'too dry'. 'Wet' characters are looser in form and characterized by sweeping brushstrokes, and spatters or splashes of ink, while 'dry' characters are precise in their shape. The calligrapher's brush itself is a complex and subtle tool. Bristles

As a backdrop for exotic items, the potency of white walls is unrivalled. The crimson colour bordering the calligraphy of this hanging scroll immediately draws the eye across the dazzling white space.

are chosen from among animal hairs, rabbit, badger, hare and weasel being the traditional favourites. Most prized of all are mouse whiskers, which are said to create brush strokes so delicate that they are almost invisible.

Ink sticks, ink stones, brushes and paper of old were crafted with such skill that they were treated as luxury items. They were produced with exquisite stylistic features that carried a strong artistic appeal. Ink stones were the crowning glory of the calligrapher's tools, made from pieces of fine-grained stone or ceramics that were etched, carved or moulded into refined shapes. Sometimes ink stones were moulded from clay that had been repeatedly filtered and washed to sift away the sediment and coarser grains before being cast into shape. An ink stone's surface looks deceptively smooth but is mildly abrasive, sloping into a shallow well into which the calligrapher dips the brush. With these tools and media the calligrapher trained for half a lifetime until he achieved virtuosity worthy of his master's approval.

Calligraphy has played an important role throughout thousands of years of Chinese civilization, when it has been viewed as both an art form and a source of cultural history. Because the legacy of the past is expressed though the written character, there is personal and public reverence for writing, which explains why calligraphy is the most venerated art form in China today. Though Western painting and literature are becoming increasingly popular in China, the passion for calligraphy still persists.

Below left Calligraphy brushes and inks like these are easily obtainable in the West and can be used on paper to imitate Chinese characters or create minimal monochrome landscapes and abstract images. *Opposite* The verbal and the visual are intertwined in the Chinese tradition, where writing is only one step away from painting. Just as Western artists often ground their work in historical techniques, the influence of classical calligraphy enters the work of many contemporary Chinese artists. Here, the double happiness symbol has been drawn in brush strokes charged with a vitality and exhilaration that capture the essence of shared joy.

CERAMICS

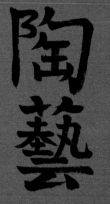

陶藝

CERAMICS

Taken from the earth and formed by fire, ceramics are regarded by the Chinese as an expression of nature itself, enhancing the natural elements provided by the wood and stone of the interior. That is not to say that Chinese ceramics are not works of great beauty – in fact, their forms have been perfected over thousands of years to balance their esoteric and aesthetic features against their functional uses.

Simply decorated with birds, animals and flowers, early ceramics celebrated the natural world by reflecting the purity of colours and contours observed in nature. Over the years they evolved into an art form that expressed figures, animals and deities in clay, culminating in the funerary objects of the Tang period. Whether glazed in simple hues of celadon or lavishly decorated with the motifs of the Qing era, Chinese ceramics are charged with a vitality that mimics that of life itself.

The Chinese trace the history of their ceramics back nine thousand years, when early potters learned to transform the basic elements of fire, earth and water into objects that were both beautiful and functional. The Neolithic Chinese tribes sculpted pottery into slender drinking vessels, and also a type of jug with a handle, a pouring spout and three hollow legs that served as a tripod base, used for heating liquids. The surfaces were marked with simple patterns and geometric designs, or were painted with flowers, fish, animals and human faces, decorations that are still popular in China today.

The potter's wheel was in use by time of the ancient Longshan culture (c.2,500 BC), believed to have been the first to make white pottery. Even more spectacular are the black ceramics they produced, the pieces of which are eggshell thin and exquisitely crafted. They were sculpted from clay coiled into ropes and carefully smoothed into shape, then fired in the ground and burnished with pebbles. These black wares are believed to be some of the most beautiful ever produced in China's history, unrivalled until the development of porcelain some three thousand years later. Although porcelain originated in the Han dynasty, the oldest existing porcelain found intact is the ivory-coloured 'white *ding*', which dates back to the seventh century.

The ceramics of the Tang dynasty were cast in rich colours, being the first multi-coloured wares in China. The style was characterized by cylindrical shapes of various proportions, but ceramic production during this period was dominated by the funerary objects entombed with the dead. Tang burial customs dictated that clay replicas of material possessions, animals and people be placed in the tomb to serve the deceased in the afterlife. Human figures representing the deceased's family and servants, sculptures of horses and pets, miniature furniture and even replicas of the house itself were cast in ceramic. The surviving Tang tomb figures are often sculptural in appearance. Camels and horses with grooms and riders, polo players, musicians, overdressed merchants and voluptuous courtesans were crafted in stunning detail. Wide-eyed warriors were made to stand guard against evil spirits, protecting the living from the superstitions that followed them into the afterlife. Most human figures were made standing atop a pedestal, though some were portrayed on horseback or participating in sport. The type of clay used and the colour of the glazes were stipulated by burial laws, and the figures' embroidered

sleeves, long robes, headdress, shoes and office or military emblems would have been made in accordance with court protocol. In keeping with their professional roles, the figures generally bore stern, somewhat remote expressions, their faces shaped with frowning mouths and glaring eyes. Their refinement and realism exemplify the artistic production of the Tang dynasty, an era of political stability and artistic achievement. Many funerary figures from the first dynasties have survived, enabling historians to trace the evolution of styles of dress, furniture and even architecture throughout the centuries.

The size and number of clay objects interred with the dead were not determined by wealth alone; they were stipulated by a complex code of burial laws. The famous life-sized terracotta figures of horses and warriors found at the tomb site of Qin Shihuangdi, the first emperor of China, are the most famous examples – only the emperor was allowed to take an entire army into the afterlife. The scale of the human figures made to represent the dead was also an indication of nobility and rank.

Ceramic funerary figures are thought to be the earliest examples of Chinese three-dimensional figurative art, inspiring the creation of decorative porcelain figurines made in later dynasties. In the early Qing dynasty, ceramic figures were made independently of funerary or religious use, although they still retained the symbolic meanings given to them in Taoism or Buddhism. Tomb figures from the late Ming dynasty later served as models for chinoiserie exports during the late seventeenth and eighteenth centuries, when the figures that were produced during the reign of the Emperor Kangxi became highly prized in the West.

The tones of blue, red and green that characterized Chinese ceramics for centuries appeared during the Song period. Foreign merchants imported a type of blue cobalt that stayed true during firing, creating blue monochrome ceramics and a pigment later used for fine detailing. The lustrous blood-red glazes of this era continued to be popular in successive dynasties, until the secret formula was lost during the sixteenth century. The green Song glazes resulted from attempts to reproduce the colour and texture of jade in ceramic to create a faux jade artefact. This had been a continuing goal of generations of Chinese craftsmen, because the sacred jade was considered a symbol of immortality. These hues of green became known in the West as celadon, and were enormously popular among European collectors throughout the eighteenth century. While the unfired glaze is greyish-green, the final product may be tinged with yellow, aubergine, turquoise or blue.

During the Song dynasty, ceramics were produced for a highly literate and intellectually elite class, resulting in many pieces that are now regarded as classics by the Chinese. With their purity of form and brilliant glazes, they exemplify a perfect balance between vitality and refinement. Monochrome pieces were thought to be especially elegant, introducing a vogue for minimalism that prevailed throughout the Yuan and Ming dynasties. The aesthetic demands of the ruling elite motivated craftsmen to progress and refine their technical skills.

Despite the popularity of coloured glazes, the combination of cobalt blue against a white background that emerged during the Yuan dynasty was to become a classic motif. Blue-and-white wares were exported in huge quantities via the Silk Route

Page 173 Like the rest of modern Chinese design, ceramics are steeped in a rich tradition that continues to draw upon classical pieces, or create expressive abstract shapes as artisans come up with new forms and pioneer new techniques. This incense burner is appliquéd with a gold rose and coated with a high gloss; its lime colour reflects the vibrant palette used in China today.

throughout the Yuan and Ming periods to Arab cultures who believed that the blue-and-white porcelain would reveal the presence of poison by turning the food served in it black. The blue-and-white style survives today, and is undoubtedly one of the oldest continuously produced porcelains ever created.

Chinese porcelain reached its artistic peak in the latter part of the fifteenth century, during the Ming dynasty. This was largely due to the discovery of new glazing techniques that enabled ceramicists to apply pigments after the piece had been fired. Deep monochromes in copper red, charcoal and dark blue followed, given lustre by the application of a clear glaze. The classic trio of yellow, green and burgundy also appeared; examples are referred to today as Ming tricolour wares. Ceramics made in multiple colour combinations are uniformly described as 'five-colour', irrespective of the actual number of colours used. Beautiful two-toned wares were thought to be the height of elegance: green-glazed patterns drawn against a yellow background, yellow glazes juxtaposed with blue, and green glazes fired over deep red were used on a wide variety of designs. The birth of colour during the Ming dynasty fired the imaginations of future artists more than in any other period.

Artistic innovation was less evident in the Qing dynasty, as emphasis was placed on new standards of quality and technical perfection. The imperial kilns in Jingdezhen advanced all forms of ceramics, reproducing the classical wares of previous eras in stronger, thinner porcelain, with perfect glazes and true colours. Porcelain masters began to paint highly detailed pictorial compositions on their wares, replacing the early motifs of flowers and animals with religious scenes, landscapes and still lifes. New technical innovations enabled them to use a wider range of colours and apply them in a variety of tones. As export trade with Europe increased during the Qing dynasty, these fine ceramics came to the attention of the West, influencing the type of porcelain produced in Europe from the mid-eighteenth century onwards.

The enamelled porcelain known in the West as *famille vert* and *famille rose* was produced in the Qing kilns mainly for export from the late seventeenth and the early eighteenth centuries respectively, and is today considered by many to be the highest form of Chinese overglazed porcelain. The polychrome painted decoration was usually floral.

The earthenware produced in China was always described using the Western terms of ceramics, pottery, porcelain and china, which are easily confused. The term 'ceramic' describes the general art of firing clay to create an ornamental or functional object, meaning that all pottery, porcelain and china can be considered ceramics. Pottery generally refers to robust wares made from porous clay that rarely has the strength or refinement of porcelain. Pottery is fired at temperatures ranging from direct sunlight to the heat of a baker's oven, or the intense heat of a kiln reaching 1100°C (about 2000°F). Pigments or colours are generally added before firing, but afterwards pottery usually remains porous enough to absorb colour.

Porcelain, on the other hand, can only be created from fine clays fired at searing temperatures between 1200° and 1400°C (about 2200°–2550°F). This high heat creates a chemical change in the clay that vitrifies it into a white glassy body with roughly the density of glass. Porcelain can be decorated after the initial firing in a range of colours and glazes, then fired again at a low temperature to seal the colour and harden the glaze. Once it has cooled, true porcelain will ring with a sonorous tone when tapped; and if it did not vitrify entirely, it will fracture into smooth pieces.

The 'china' we refer to in the English language initially distinguished fine Chinese porcelain from that manufactured in Europe, but today this distinction is not made. The plates, bowls, cups and vases commonly referred to as china today describe a wide range of everyday items, with the term porcelain often refering to something more luxurious. There are many more distinctions between them, and many different grades of quality within the two categories.

Different grades are determined by a number of factors, the most significant of them being the type of clay. Chinese soil is rich in clay, with large deposits of ochre-coloured loess in the north, referred to by the Chinese as yellow earth. The silt of these deposits washes into the Yellow River, producing its distinctive colour. Historically, ceramicists were restricted to using clay quarried locally as loess is not suitable for ceramics, and this is why the best ceramic workshops were established where the best clay was found. The towns of Yixing and Jingdezhen, for example, became the foremost producers of fine porcelain, because there was a plentiful supply of superior-quality clay in the area. Today, high-quality ceramics are made from blends containing several types of clay from different regions, even in the porcelain workshops of Yixing and Jingdezhen.

The most popular clay in these regions is kaolin, or china clay, the hard, white earth that results from the decomposition of granite-bearing rock. Used in China since the seventh century, kaolin is the main ingredient in hard-paste porcelain. Deposits were discovered in Germany and used at Meissen, making it the first factory in Europe to produce true porcelain. In Britain, the pure white porcelain known as bone china takes its name from the added ingredient of bone ash. This is the predominant form of ceramic made in Britain today, based on a formula created at the Spode factory in the late eighteenth century.

With the outbreak of World War II, all kilns were closed and ceramic production ground to a halt until peace was declared in 1945. The state-operated factories in Jingdezhen were reopened and have recently been transformed into private potteries, rapidly regaining some of their former glory. Foreign artists are now flooding into China to study traditional ceramics, as well as painting, calligraphy and sculpture. The fusion of East and West is changing the form and style of China's ceramic tradition, expanding the scope of colour and material used by Chinese ceramicists. Key exhibitions curated in Beijing and Shanghai's major galleries are touring the world to showcase the talent of Chinese ceramicists, to international acclaim. There is now a sculptural dimension in many contemporary Chinese ceramics, inspired by avant-garde and pop art movements in the West, using traditional practices to express contemporary meaning.

Today's industry heralds a renaissance for Chinese ceramics, with reproductions produced to unsurpassed standards, and contemporary Chinese designs gaining recognition throughout the world. Drawing on its rich heritage of ceramics, China is now creating designs that reflect both streamlined decoration and austere functionality, bringing art and history into the mundane aspects of everyday life.

The shapes and forms of Chinese ceramics have changed little throughout China's long decorative history. Many of the shapes shown here remain contemporary today, and these same glazes continue to be reproduced in provincial kilns. Light blue colours and greenish celadon hues are among the oldest glazes used by Chinese ceramicists; they often created a 'washed' effect after firing, as these rustic pieces illustrate. Chinese colour glazes reached their peak in the Qing dynasty when advances in science enabled ceramicists to use minerals that yielded lasting colours and lustrous finishes.

Pattern & Motif

Like the rest of the Chinese decorative arts, the decoration on the ceramics was not to be taken lightly. Before the Qing dynasty, ceramics relied mainly on style and form for aesthetic appeal; the depiction of deities, sacred symbols, mystic signs and mythological animals designated functional ceramics and ritual objects. A Taoist devotee would have displayed a vase depicting the goddess Xiwangmu, the legendary 'Queen Mother of the West', holding a double gourd as a symbol of her ability to foretell the future, to attest to the promise of riches to come. A wine cup depicting a basket of lilies and *lingshi* – a type of fungus associated with immortality or long life – would be a literal means of drinking to one's health. Almost any series of animals portrayed in fives is emblematic of the 'five blessings': long life, riches, peace, love of virtue and a venerated end to one's life. These abound on platters, bowls and vases from the Han dynasty to the present day.

Early eighteenth-century porcelain masters in the West tried to imitate the elegant symbols and motifs of the ceramics made during the reign of Emperor Kangxi, but succumbed to the pervasive pressure of the Baroque. A vogue for the elegant depictions of willowy ladies known as 'Long Elizas' (a corruption of the Dutch term for them, Lange Lijzen) that featured on some eighteenth-century Kangxi blue-and-white porcelain swept through Europe and America, and the designs were copied by Worcester and by manufacturers of delftware. In the nineteenth century, prevailing tastes moved away from chinoiserie and towards Neoclassical designs. It then became possible to make most of these in Europe, since the technical knowledge developed during the Qing era had also been exported to the West. As the industry in Europe grew, the great porcelain factories of Sèvres, Limoges, Staffordshire and Delft became renowned for their sets of china, fine teapots, ceramic tiles and refined vases. Their quality paralleled the works produced in China, but lacked the spirituality fundamental to Chinese ceramics.

East and West were finally bridged at the beginning of the twentieth century by the work of the late Bernard Leach, Britain's leading studio ceramicist and an influential international master. Leach grew up in the Far East; he was born in Hong Kong of British parents and lived in Japan before coming to Britain in 1920. Initially known for his Japanese style, Leach was a purist who combined elements of Eastern and Western practices, designs and glazes. The influence of his work elevated the status of the Western potter to that of an artist rather than a craftsman. Leach charged clay with the feeling and finesse associated with fine art, describing his engagement with the materials as an artistic process. As critics drew parallels between his pieces and sculptural forms, ceramics was established as a discipline of the arts. Leach's works, and those of his wife and son, are today regarded as art pieces and sought after by museums and collectors.

Leach's forte was his ability to paint designs freehand in the traditional Chinese method, using a fine brush to render motifs and to outline the features of the vase. The Chinese also use stencils for ornate detailing like patterns and medallions. Pigments are powdered and blown onto the surface through the stencil using a bamboo tube, then left to dry. The stencil is then removed and further ornamentation applied, painted smoothly and continuously with a brush containing no more paint than can be immediately absorbed. The entire surface is then coated with a clear glaze and fired.

This beautiful gold-rimmed porcelain plate by De Gournay is hand-turned and hand-painted. It features a pseudo tobacco-leaf pattern that imitates the Chinese export porcelain produced in the second half of the eighteenth century. Its 'orange peel' glaze gives it a slightly uneven coating, which makes it look and feel like an antique plate.

Glazes

Chinese glazes are admired throughout the world for their spectacular colours and finishes – not least in China itself where they have been poetically compared to 'the rising moon', 'breaking river ice' and the 'colour of the sky after the rain'. Some Chinese glazes are bright and lustrous in tone, imitating the brilliance of precious gems or shimmering water, while others are deep, multifaceted and subtle, with hues that appear to change along with the ambient light. Glazes could be applied by dipping the entire ceramic into the solution, or washing it with a brush, or slowly dripping it down the sides of the vase so that it stopped just short of the base. Such simple monochromatic glazes were always pleasing to the cultivated Chinese taste.

The story of glazes is also the story of Chinese ceramics itself. The potters of ancient China worked miracles, transforming simple materials into coloured finishes, making high-fired glazed ceramics in beiges and browns. *Ding* ceramics evolved out of conscious attempts to produce a pure white clay body. White, translucent and unporous, the unfired *ding* forms easily lent themselves to the application of dense glazes or 'wash' methods. As well as the famous white *ding*, with its ivory glaze and unglazed rim (usually bound with metal), there were black, purple and red forms. Some of the burnished caramel colours of black *ding* have surfaces so dark and dense that they glint with the aura of polished ebony. What was initially regarded as the colour 'black' has since proved to be a cunning optical illusion resulting from coating scorched clay with opaque coffee-brown glazes; true black appeared only much later, in the Qing dynasty. Early potters created special effects by spattering the glaze with ash and straw, or painstakingly imitating tortoiseshell patterns, the fine striations of hare's fur, and the textured mottling of partridge feathers.

The intense, high-fired glazes used in China today trace their origins all the way back to Bronze Age wares, as high-fired glazes are known to have been used on stoneware as early as the Shang dynasty. Roughly two millennia later, the Song dynasty's wonderfully refined monochrome glazes were perfectly complemented by the undecorated earthenware in simple, classic shapes.

The potters of the early Ming dynasty perfected ferrous red and cobalt blue glazes, luring tastes away from the darker, more austere ceramics of old (though dark-glazed ceramics have been making a quiet comeback in the West in recent years).

The body and glaze of the distinctive blue-and-white Ming ceramics gradually changed over the three centuries of the Ming period. The glazed bases of early Ming pieces tend to be mottled and uneven, with thicker foot rims than those of the mid- and late Ming period. Most glazes appeared heavier and less translucent during the early years of the dynasty, gradually evolving to the transparent glazes of the late Ming period.

The glazes and decorations developed at the imperial kilns of the Qing dynasty were intended to reproduce natural colours by achieving a precise balance of minerals, firing temperature and timing. During the Kangxi reign, copper oxide was introduced as a colorant to create the red hues of the '*sang de boeuf*' glaze and the pale pink 'peach bloom' glaze, which darkens and pales like a ripening peach. Also developed during the Kangxi reign, the light blue glaze known as '*clair de lune*' has always been one of the most treasured of Qing glazes, and was reserved exclusively for imperial porcelains.

As the use of colour evolved during the Tang dynasty, it created a basic palette for subsequent eras to explore. These Tang wine cups were fired with the *sancai* glaze, later paralleled in the distinctive combination of green, yellow and burgundy that characterized Ming tricolour wares. Though many refined and stylized designs were produced by the Ming kilns, the understated beauty of rustic pieces like these is still appealing today.

Forms

Just as Chinese calligraphy became the world's earliest abstract drawing, by medieval times Chinese ceramics were perhaps the earliest abstract sculptures. Based on the expression of pure form and understated colour, their shapes were borrowed from ancient bronzes dating back thousands of years. These vessels were cast in bold sculptural forms with a functional purpose in mind, and ornamentation and detailing were kept to a minimum. Over time, rich glazes, colours and motifs began to decorate their surfaces, but the striking simplicity of their forms prevailed. The effect created a sense of complex harmony in form rather than a simple balance of decoration; a principle applied to many features of modern design today.

Chinese ceramicists are distinct from their Western counterparts, most markedly in their preservation of classical designs. The Chinese have a long tradition of venerating simple, rounded forms combined with subtle glazes. Though these pieces are essentially functional objects, they can also be appreciated for the sense of balance and precision which they convey.

Modern Chinese ceramics are characterized by the purity and strength associated with classical forms, but their shapes are often abstractly thrown or constructed to suit functional needs. Many of the modern vertical shapes have long, sinuous necks that merge into a broad base, or wide mouths that narrow into a rounded belly. Others can be squarish in shape, with wide necks that sit atop spreading 'shoulders' contoured into the base. Vases may have delicate rims that are flaring or fluted, or distinctive forked mouths. These recall the fine silver and bronze vessels from the Song dynasty that feature complex flower-shaped mouths astride tightly constricted necks. The effect is both delicate and exotic, but notoriously difficult to produce, even today.

The classic ovoid, or egg-shaped, form also emerged during the Song period. The ovoid shape was perfected by highly skilled craftsmen who laboured at the potter's wheel for hours to tease hollow contours out of the bulbous clay. Ovoid shapes were dexterously stretched into a vase or flattened into a dish, and used as decanters and jars. Conical bowls and vases are also associated with this period, many characterized by the deliberate contrasts between their inner and outer surfaces.

Chinese relief decoration on ceramics has always rendered texture and depth, presented contrasts and created a sense of variety. Throughout history it has featured brilliant combinations of imaginary creatures, including coiled dragons, scrolling cloud patterns, breaking waves and pools of water swirling in gentle spirals. Chinese ceramicists deftly applied vertical or spiral ribs of clay in order to create even more strongly contrasting lines, and traced the rims and necks of lateral pieces with delicate thread moulding.

Beyond the commercially labelled 'Made in China' ceramics are beautifully crafted one-off, hand-thrown pieces. These ceramics are usually organic in shape and texture, and are crafted as an expression of form rather than as a surface for decoration. Made mostly in provincial workshops, ceramics like these, which are rarely exported, are known mainly among the most esoteric dealers. Their shapes are cool, understated and thoroughly modern, and tend to be of a richer, darker lustre than the light tones that are currently favoured in the West.

The tubed jar (far right) dates from the Song dynasty, its lustre emanating from a China-*pai* glaze applied many centuries ago. The tall urn shown beside it is a Tang amphora; used to hold grain wine or water, it is crafted with handles that transform into dragon's heads as they dip into its spout. The amphora's main body is unadorned except for the ribs of clay applied to define the neck and lip. The vase on its left dates from the Ming dynasty. It was shaped by incising the clay rather than adding ribs, with a cheeky dragon making a whimsical decoration as it winds around the neck of the vase. The symmetry of the crackle-glazed celadon vase (far left) balances two contoured shapes on either side of a hollow orb.

Page 184 Early pottery was sculpted into vessels and jugs with handles and pouring spouts. Their surfaces were simply decorated with birds, animals, flowers and other symbols from the natural world, or with bold patterns. The piece shown here was painted with curving lines that arc around the medallions drawn in their centre. Designs like this have inspired ceramicists today to paint designs freehand, using fine brushes to create motifs and outline the integral features.

Page 185 China produces a wide variety of ceramics, ranging from fine porcelain pieces made in factories to rustic earthenware containers fired in a village kiln. Although pottery generally refers to robust wares made from porous clay, the term is also used to describe the rare, hand-thrown pieces with organic shapes and finishes crafted in provincial workshops, like the bowls shown here.

Above These contemporary white porcelain pieces eschew superfluous decoration and rely upon their streamlined shapes and gentle textures to project a unique aesthetic.

Opposite Rustic pieces provide the perfect elements of contrast in a minimal interior. Set atop a sleek fireplace, their round bowls and wide necks add gentle contours that balance the harsh right angles dominating this part of the room. The white surroundings enhance the subtle tones of blue and grey in their glazes and highlight the shadows cast by their sculptural forms.

Buying antiques

Chinese antiques are often auctioned in the major cities of Europe and North America. Attending auctions is a good way of appraising the market, and auctioneers can sometimes broker deals between collectors on items that have not yet been booked for auction. If you decide to buy a period piece as an investment, it is worth visiting dealers to compare prices and ranges of merchandise. The advantage of buying from dealers is that their antiques are usually sold in pristine condition; if not, they can arrange for a professional conservator to carry out the work needed. But whether buying from an auctioneer or an antique dealer, question the provenance and ask for certificates of authenticity – before handing the money over.

Serious collectors travel to Beijing, Shanghai and Hong Kong to look for rare items and competitive prices. All antique dealers must guarantee the quality of their goods in accordance with laws passed to protect the interests of foreign collectors. As buyers are legally obliged to have their purchases appraised by the customs office (which most international shipping companies arrange on their client's behalf), the government can identify any fakes and arrange to take the appropriate action against the dealer. Note that Chinese law currently forbids export of any antique older than three hundred years if it has been crafted from the precious *zitan*, *huanghuali* or *jichimu* woods. As laws change, it is advisable that collectors get advice before purchasing to ensure that they will be allowed to take them home.

Chronology

Xia dynasty	c.1900–c.1550BC	Tang dynasty	618–907
Shang dynasty	c.1550–c.1050BC	Five Dynasties period	907–960
Zhou dynasty	c.1050–256BC	Song dynasty	960–1279
Qin dynasty	221–206BC	Yuan dynasty	1279–1368
Han dynasty	206BC–AD220	Ming dynasty	1368–1644
Three Kingdoms period	220–265	Qing dynasty	1644–1911
Six Dynasties period	265–589	Republic of China established	1912
Sui dynasty	589–618	People's Republic of China established	1949

Index

The author and publisher would like to thank the following for the loan of locations and material for photography:

Agent Provocateur 16 Pont Street, Knightsbridge, London SW1 020 7235 0229 www.agentprovocateur.com **101 top left and bottom right, 124**
Bam-Bou restaurant and bar, 1 Percy Street London W1P 0ET 020 7323 9140 www.bam-bou.co.uk **19, 89, 90**
Eileen Coyne, specialist painter 020 8741 1764: Graham Collins Design 020 8671 5356: **30, 133**
Neisha Crossland: wallpaper **72 top**
De Gournay 112 Old Church Street, London SW3 6EP: curtain **5**, wallpaper **9, 66, 71, 72, bottom 73, 86** wallpaper and china **75, 179** throw **111** china figures **153**
General Trading Company, cafe designed by Spencer Fung **58**
Josette Plismy/Gong **32–33, 81, 99**
Rabhi Hage: furniture **129**
Hakkasan restaurant, designer: Christian Liagre **22, 77**
Kirsten Heckterman: fabric **116–117, 125 top left** cushion **136 left**

Katie Jones 195 Westbourne Grove, London W11 2SB, bowls designed by Robert Kuo **155, 156 top right**
Kelaty: carpet **16–17, 130–131**
Mirabelle **72 bottom**
Nom: furniture and tableware **57** tray **85**
Mimmi O'Connell Port of Call 020 7589 4836: **27, 31 101 top right and bottom left, 146 right** wooden plates **61** trunk **140–141**
Yves Ogier: location and materials **1**, posters **68, 163** cushion and chair **88** lacquerware from Ogier, table by Florence Bandoux from Oom Collection **156 bottom right**
Ormonde Gallery: ink stone and inkblock **150** snuff bottles and display case **165** ceramics **181, 183, 184**
Ornamenta: wallpaper **105 right**
Patara: designer: Ou Baholyodhin **6, 83, 104** Hong Kong chair by Ou Baholyodhin **6**
Sarah Pavey **147**
Phillip Quiggly: cushions **80, 125 bottom right**
Sally Rigg: ceramics **187**
David Robson Architects **129**
Scalamandre: wallpaper **74, 95** fabric and cushion **113**

Shanghai Tang 6a/b Sloane Street, London SW1 9LE www.shanghaitang.com: **24, 82, 107** tea pot, cups and tray: **62–63** notebook **109** fabric **122–123**
Shanxi 020 7498 7611: cabinet **2**, vase: **37** furniture **92–93, 95, 105, 112, 113, 115** furniture and hatbox **109** chair **111**
Soo San 598a Kings Road, London SW6 2DX: location and furniture **25** poster **29** carpet **127, 129** location **145, 156 top left, 177** figures **146 left** spectacle cases **150**
Rupert Spira: ceramic **170–171**
Peter Ting: Hiberne Chine 020 7274 8900 **38, 56, 60, 78–79, 119, 143, 151–152, 157, 164, 167** incense burner **173**
Ushida Finlay Architects: **26, 39, 54, 111, 156 bottom left**
Vessel: spoon **179**
Edmund de Wall: ceramics **186**
Linda Wrigglesworth: altar scroll **57** altar cushion **137** fan cases **161**
Bosenquett Yves: carpet **127**

Acknowledgements

I would like to thank those who have influenced the content of this book: Paola Zamperini for her accounts of Qing dynasty urban life; Nancy Berliner for her exhaustive research on Chinese vernacular furniture; Dawn Jacobs for her texts on chinoiserie; Vivienne Tam for her accounts of life in China and Hong Kong; and the American sinologist and historian John S. Major, senior lecturer at The China Institute, New York, and author of many books on Chinese history, whose critique vastly improved the manuscript.

I would also like to express my gratitude to the museums and institutions that facilitated my research: the Far Eastern Department at the Victoria and Albert Museum, London, especially for providing Craig Clunas' study of classical Chinese furniture and Verity Wilson's texts on Chinese costume and textiles; the librarians, photographic archivists, keepers and curators of the Classical China, Qing China and Lacquer collections, Musée Guimet, Paris; the Far Eastern Department at the Metropolitan Museum of Art, New York, especially for texts on the Astor court and the Chinese Decorative Arts collection; the librarians at the School of Oriental and African Studies, University of London; the Percival David Foundation, University of London; and the History of Art Department, Birkbeck College, University of London.

My thanks to Jan Baldwin for her beautiful photography, Lindsay Milne for her resourcefulness, Megan Smith and Lucy Gowans for their art direction and Alison Wormleighton for her helpful comments. Above all, I would like to thank the editor, Muna Reyal, for her vision, enthusiasm and encouragement. For their support and contributions, I am grateful to Ana Avalon, Bo Madestrand, Deleah Shaffer, Ingela Hedlund Claxton, Hélène Armstrong, Kathryn Earle, Michel Andenmatten, Marc Blane, Maria Friberg, Mark Forman, Simon Su, Su Ling Wang and Yeohlee Tan. A special thank you to Kate Haxell for suggesting me in the first place.

The Publisher would like to thank the following photographers and organisations for their kind permission to reproduce the photographs in this book:
10 Christie's Images; 11 Christie's Images; 13 John Thomson, 1869/Wellcome Library, London; 14 Christie's Images; 15 Christie's Images; 21 Hutchison Picture Library; 23 Courtesy of the Trustees of the Victoria and Albert Museum, London; 35 Courtesy of the Trustees of the Victoria and Albert Museum, London; 42 Photos12.com – OIP; 139 Christie's Images; 159 Courtesy of the Trustrees of the Victoria and Albert Museum, London